THE PINE FURNITURE OF
EARLY NEW ENGLAND

THE

PINE FURNITURE

of *Early New England*

RUSSELL HAWES KETTELL

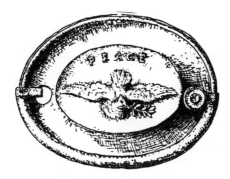

WITH 284 ILLUSTRATIONS

Dover Publications, Inc.

NEW YORK

Published in Canada by General Publishing Company, Ltd., 30 Lesmill Road, Don Mills, Toronto, Ontario.
Published in the United Kingdom by Constable and Company, Ltd., 10 Orange Street, London WC 2.

This Dover edition, first published in 1949, is an unabridged and unaltered republication of the work originally published in 1929 by Doubleday, Doran and Company. This edition is published by special arrangement with Doubleday and Company, Inc.

International Standard Book Number: 0-486-20145-7

Library of Congress Catalog Card Number: 59-11843

Manufactured in the United States of America
Dover Publications, Inc.
180 Varick Street
New York, N.Y. 10014

THIS BOOK IS AFFECTIONATELY DEDICATED TO MY MOTHER

WHOSE INTEREST IN THIS, AS IN ALL MY VENTURES

WAS NEVER LESS THAN MY OWN

CONTENTS

FOREWORD

A STUDY of the woodwork of past centuries shows that elementary methods of construction were either evolved and handed down or rediscovered by skilled craftsmen of all ages. The dove-tailed joint was used in Egyptian sarcophagi five thousand years ago, and the mortise and tenon is seen in the furniture of ancient Greece. The joinery of the Eighteenth Century was adequate for the complex creations of French and English designers, and the work "stood up." There is pleasure in the contemplation of even the most simple object of craftsmanship in which traditional methods of construction serve the best interests of the material, the maker, and the owner. A great wealth of satisfaction has been widespread among a people when common objects represented much in human skill and what might be called "a common-sense-ingenuity," and hence our recurring and active interest in folk-art.

It is significant in this connection that, even aside from educational or æsthetic points of view, modern research has realized the need of the combined exercise of the mind, the hand, and the eye. An age-old custom becomes with us a game contributing toward mental and bodily health, and occupational therapy is one answer to a recognized need in present day life. When a "scientifically perfected age" offers us standardized course-dinners assembled through the economic bargain of quantity production there will always remain the enthusiast who will find joy in preparing meat and drink over his own fire—even a wood-fire. We believe there is an analogy between this and the ways of the knowing craftsman of to-day who prefers to remain an amateur through his love of the game. He is the impractical fellow who still harbours the fine spirit of fending for himself, at least in personal matters. The interesting objects of more or less homespun variety shown in the following pages were personal matters, for they were made by individuals for individuals, and they smack of the directness and independence of spirit of those who honour their own place in life.

That these objects do not represent "the last word" in furniture making it is needless to say: but they do represent more nearly the first word in American craftsmanship. Such furniture filled a real need once upon a time, and under appropriate circumstances the same need can be met in the same spirit, for all good furniture is derivative in design. Mr. Kettell, with a fine regard for his subject, has devoted years of careful study and disinterested effort in bringing together the examples and the drawings shown in this volume.

EDWIN J. HIPKISS

ACKNOWLEDGMENTS

THE WRITER *wishes to make it very plain that without the generous attitude of a great many people such a book as this could never have been assembled.*

First of all, he wishes to thank the owners of the examples illustrated for coöperating so freely with him in the idea of the book. If a knowledge of these early New England pieces and how to arrange them congenially in an architectural setting is spread among an interested group of collectors, the owners of the houses into which the writer's camera was allowed to intrude may feel very largely the satisfaction of responsibility.

To Mr. Henry W. Erving, the writer wishes to make a very especial acknowledgment. His kindly, expert, and generous interest has been woven into the fabric of the writing from the first page to the last.

Other men have given much appreciated assistance. The writer, therefore, welcomes this opportunity of expressing publicly his thanks to Mr. Edwin J. Hipkiss, Mr. Henry Davis Sleeper, Mr. Henry W. Kent, Mr. Charles O. Cornellius, Mr. William Cordingly, Mr. George Francis Dow, Mr. William Sumner Appleton, Professor Richard T. Fisher, Professor Irving W. Bailey, and the writer's architectural associates, Messrs. Strickland, Blodget, and Law. Mr. William C. Vaughan was generous in offering the use of his material pertaining to hardware.

Practically all of these beautiful drawings were made by Mr. Nils Alsen, Mr. Albert Hoedtke, and Mr. Walter Macomber; while the credit for the photographic results, in nine cases out of ten, belongs to the mysterious focussing and calculating of Mr. Charles Darling.

Among the photographs and drawings, any pieces not otherwise accredited belong to the writer. Many of these were photographed against "borrowed" backgrounds, frequently in the Browne House at Watertown, because the writer does not happen to live in a house built in the Seventeenth or Eighteenth Century.

ILLUSTRATIONS

From photographs

ILLUSTRATIONS *from Photographs*

ILLUSTRATIONS *from Photographs*

ILLUSTRATIONS *from Photographs*

ILLUSTRATIONS *from Photographs*

ILLUSTRATIONS *from Photographs*

ILLUSTRATIONS *from Photographs*

MIRRORS

ILLUSTRATIONS *from Photographs*

ILLUSTRATIONS *from Photographs*

ILLUSTRATIONS

From Drawings

ILLUSTRATIONS *from Drawings*

THE PINE FURNITURE OF
EARLY NEW ENGLAND

INTRODUCTION

THE PURPOSE of this book is twofold. First, the writer believes that a better knowledge will add greatly to one's appreciation of the beautiful, though humble, furniture that was constructed in this country during its early years. The curves, the mouldings, the admirable joinery hold many a thrill in store for those who will spare the time to examine them. It seems as if man must have a great store of the treasure that we may call beauty, which he feels in duty bound to lavish upon the work of his hands. And in an age such as that which we are considering, it was the chests, the boxes, the tables, the chairs, and the cupboards that received this treasure, for they were the most lasting things on his restricted list.

The second purpose may best be explained in this manner. Has the reader ever been to a stonecutter's and seen a workman putting his conscientious effort into some mediocre design, the product of a man higher up? Capable, perhaps of turning out a masterpiece, this workman can never get beyond the limitations of his blueprint. There is the pity of it! It is the writer's hope that he may reproduce designs that will be worthy of the effort of anyone who has a real love of making things himself, whether he be cabinetmaker, schoolboy, or business man working at home on a rainy Sunday.

Most of the pieces considered in this book were made entirely, or for the most part, of pine. Pine, a smooth-grained wood, invites graceful mouldings and free-swinging curves, and it wears away at projecting edges and corners until the table top or wainscot has an interesting texture that can be duplicated in no other material. Furthermore, the ease with which the wood can be worked has led craftsmen into all sorts of ingenious pieces of joinery that for long left nails only a secondary function, or eliminated them.

Probably it is the spirit of frank simplicity that gives this work its fundamental appeal. It is on friendly terms with open fires, with wrought-iron hinges, with hewn beams and corner posts, with rough-plastered walls or robin's-egg blue panelling and wide board flooring painted pumpkin yellow. All these things speak the same language.

But 'ware lest you introduce a piece of mahogany to such a company! The mahogany raises its eyebrows at favourite scratches and rounded edges of the pine, while the pine peeks out of the corners of its eyes at the painstaking satinwood inlay and wonders what it is all about.

I. MATERIAL

FOR LUMBERING PURPOSES all the woods of the world are divided into two classes—the hard woods and the soft woods. Among the former are placed the broad-leaved trees, mostly deciduous, that is, those that shed their leaves in the winter. The list includes oak, elm, ash, chestnut, maple, birch, beech, walnut, apple, cherry, mahogany and many others. In the second class, the soft woods, are the conifers, most of which are evergreen. These are the hemlocks, the cedars, the spruces, the firs, and lastly, the pines.

Pines grow in a generous distribution over the northern hemisphere, reaching down into the tropics on the fingers of the mountain ranges. The typical European species, *Pinus sylvestris*, is especially plentiful in the Scandinavian peninsula. In Germany, Russia, Poland, and Siberia it abounds. But the supply which in prehistoric times grew plentifully in the British Isles, is now limited to the Highlands, where, however, some of the largest specimens may be found, measuring in some instances more than five feet in diameter.

Pine trees have always grown abundantly in the north-central and western parts of the American continent, but, with land transportation undeveloped, this source of material was not a factor in Colonial life. The typical pine tree of the Southern states is what is known in lumbering as Southern Yellow Pine, a general heading including four specific trees: long leaf, short leaf, loblolly, and Cuban. They are all, so-called, hard pines, and have a brilliant contrast in color in the grain; the quick full growth of May and June showing light, while the slower and more compact wood made during the summer months appears a reddish-brown. If the board is cut from the inside of the tree, the stripes are thin, straight, parallel; if cut from toward the outside of the trunk, the design of red and white spreads out into broad irregular patterns, best described as leaves. The soft pine, so characteristic of New England, is not an important factor in the South, growing only on the higher altitudes.

This brings us by a process of elimination to New England. Here we had, in Colonial times, both hard and soft pines in abundance. It seems to have been the hard pines that the builders first took into their confidence, probably because their standard of strength and durability and their type of construction were set by oak. There were two hard pines, much alike, and difficult (and unimportant)to distinguish, in the board, from one another. One of these, Pitch Pine, or *Pinus rigidus*, although it still grows in some localities, no longer may be considered in the market. Formerly it grew plentifully in central and southern New England and competed quite definitely with white pine for favour. The other is Red or Norway Pine, *Pinus resinosa*. It has always been common in the northern parts of New England and is still cut in moderate quantities. Its weight is given as thirty-one pounds per cubic foot. The tree grows to a height of seventy to ninety feet and to a diameter of two to three feet. The wood is a pale red in colour with striping suggesting that described in the Southern Yellow Pine, but much less pronounced. An old board, stained and weathered in use, may, at first, be confused with a board of soft pine, until its hardness is discovered by an investigating thumbnail. Floor boards, chest lids, and heavily framed tables found hard pine quite capable of withstanding rigorous use.

But the White Pine, *Pinus strobus*, played the lead. Its soft yet durable wood, surprisingly free from knots, was found to last almost as well as oak, and, with some alterations in the designs, to be perfectly suitable for the use of furniture and wainscotting.

Its weight per cubic foot is but twenty-seven pounds. The tree grows to a height of from one hundred to one hundred and twenty feet, and sometimes considerably more, while the diameters run from two to four and even five feet. The wood is light, soft, and straight grained, of medium strength and elasticity. In color it is a light brown, almost a cream, that turns the most astonishing shades under the action of time and light. Unpainted wainscot that has stood for two centuries in a north room with reduced light will often be a startling red-orange, while that exposed to the bleaching process of the sun softens in texture but remains nearly as light as it was on the day it was installed. This film of age, precious because no artificial reproduction of it is at all to be mistaken for the real thing, is called the patina.

The really big trees of both hard and soft pine have nearly vanished from New England. Old vertical sheathing we frequently see in twenty-eight inch widths, and thirty-inch table tops are often of a single board. But the sort of tree that could be squared off and cut into such surfaces must be sought for elsewhere to-day. We may occasionally see huge trees growing in a reservation, as on the Pisgab tract in Winchester, New Hampshire, which belongs to the Harvard Forest, but they now rate as museum areas, dependent upon private generosity for their preservation.

There are two soft woods, basswood and whitewood, which were used in the same way as pine and which one should be able to distinguish from it. According to the lumberman's classification, as they are deciduous trees, they should be hardwoods, but such actually is far from the case. Basswood is a light wood, soft and tough, that does not show the broad though faint graining of the pine. It was often used in chair seats. Whitewood, the market name for the wood of the tulip tree, is lighter still in weight. Uncommon north of Massachusetts, it is found to a considerable extent in the furniture of the southern New England states, particularly Connecticut. New or protected wood has a marked greenish color, and it never ages into the red and orange colors that are characteristic of old pine, nor is there any pronounced grain. Because whitewood was found to be so clear of knots, it was most favoured for use in the painted chests that are so characteristic of Connecticut.

Poplar, which also is a deciduous tree whose wood is soft, has been little used in furniture because of the difficulties experienced in seasoning the boards, and because of their tendency to warp. Its usefulness is greater in paper manufacture, and for packing cases.

Anyone thoroughly accustomed to the use of a high-powered microscope may go a considerable distance toward making a satisfactory identification of any one of the only three species of pine (white, red and pitch) that he is likely to find among the old furniture of the New England colonies. He will need, beside the microscope and a knowledge of how to handle it, considerable skill in obtaining a thin radial longitudinal section. But if he can reach the point of seeing a clear picture of the structure, the identification of it should be easy by a reference to DRAWING I in this book.

If he would rest upon the satisfaction of expert advice, this may now be obtained by sending a piece of the wood in question—a piece if possible one-quarter of an inch cube, gauged out of an unimportant surface—to the United States Forest Parks Laboratory, Madison, Wisconsin.

2. CONSTRUCTION

ALL OF THE STANDARD METHODS of joinery were common knowledge by the close of the Seventeenth Century. A man had practically the same bag of tricks as has the cabinetmaker to-day, with one point in exception—he had to perform these tricks by hand, whereas to-day there are machines to do them for him.

The crudest method of running two boards together is that known as a butt joint.(See DRAWING 2 for the types of jointing.) One board runs abruptly into the other ("abuts" it) and the joint is secured by nails. This, however, represents the very poorest kind of construction. Its two main faults are obvious. In the first place, after the least bit of warping or shrinkage or loosening, the joint is no longer tight; and in the second place it is easily pulled apart as the nails simply back out of their holes. This, in the construction of a drawer-front, for instance, would be serious.

A far better construction, and one that was used for a long time in joining the sides of drawers to the front board, is known as the shouldered corner. This provides the possibility of nailing from the side (and from the front, too, when it is desirable) and is consequently a stronger joint when subjected to a pull; it forms a snug inside corner, and it shows no construction from the front.

Somewhat similar is the housed joint which has many everyday uses in which it fears no rival. It is the accepted way of running horizontal boards into side pieces in dressers, corner cupboards, chests, and so on. In fact, whenever one board runs into another board at right angles and across its grain, the chances are it will be housed into it. It has always been common practice to sink the housed joint one third of the thickness of the board.

The plain dovetail joint was introduced in the last years of the Seventeenth Century. At first it was very crudely made, with but one or two tails to each stretch and with the intervening pins correspondingly thick. It was a useful joint, although not handsome, and we meet it in many places, first perhaps in the backs of drawers, used in conjunction with the shouldered corner, which still appeared at the front vertical edges.

It was really a combination of the good features of these two joints that produced the lap dovetail. Here we have a joint secure even without nails or glue, which is, like the shouldered corner, invisible on the front. This joint took over the responsibility of the front vertical corners of drawers, and still takes care of the problem in a thoroughly satisfactory manner. The introduction of a projecting lip (about 1725) to cover the crack around the drawer, and the refining and multiplying of the pins and tails are the only changes that have taken place.

To-day a clever cabinetmaker can make what is known as a secret, or blind dovetail joint, which appears, from both outside and inside, to be just a plain mitered joint. This is hardly more than a very clever flourish and was certainly not known in the Seventeenth or Eighteenth Centuries.

The mitered joint, just spoken of, is a familiar one, made by cutting off each board at a forty-five-degree angle. The advantages of such an arrangement are two-fold. First, the joint is neat, both inside and out, as no construction and no end grain is to be seen. Second, in the case of elaborate mouldings, as, for instance, in the carrying of a cornice around the angle of a chest of drawers, the irregular profile presents no difficulty at all. The objections to the joint are mainly that it is insecure unless nailed to a solid base, as it would be when used, as just described for the moulding of a chest. Warping is disastrous, and shrinkage in the wood causes the inside angle to open up. This form of joint, then, is resorted to in moulded cornices and frames, but seldom appears elsewhere.

One of the most useful joints of all is the mortise and tenon. Nearly always when one finds a framework construction, as opposed to a box construction, one finds the lesser members tenoned into the more solid ones, for this is the strongest method of joining.

There are three ways in which this joint was made secure. The most natural way was to drive a square peg into a hole bored through the sides of the mortise and through the tenon, too. The tenon usually is one-third the width of the post, and is set with one of its faces flush with the face of the post into which it was embedded. When the hole in the tenon is made about an eighth of an inch nearer its shoulders than it should apparently be bored, and the peg driven through, the joint is pulled up to an admirable tightness. In addition to mastering this trick, the Colonials knew that if they made the tenon piece out of well dried wood while the post with the mortise in it was of less well seasoned material, the inevitable shrinking in the latter would hold the tenon as in a vise.

When, as in certain problems, it was not practical to drive a peg in from the side, owing either to the thinness of the boards or the distance of the mortise from the edge, the tenon might be made solid by means of a wedge driven into a chisel mark, as one secures an axe head to its handle. This method is used when boards rather than sticks are joined, if their broad surfaces meet at right angles. When the broad surfaces meet in the same plane, as in the rails and stiles of a panelled door, of course the problem calls for pegs.

The third method of securing a mortise and tenon joint was to cut a slot or a hole in the tenon extending beyond the mortise and to fasten it with a wedge or pin.

If two pieces of wood cross each other, as do the legs of an "X"-trestle table, they are usually joined by what is known as a lap joint; that is, one board is simply placed or "lapped" over the other, and each cut into for half its thickness. Sometimes the joint is used at a flat corner, for it is easily made, but here a mortise and tenon joint is better and is more often used. These two forms of lap joint are often called halved joints. There is another common form of halved joint which we find used to make the fronts of chests fit snugly against the end boards.

In sheathing a room, or in forming a wide, unbroken surface from boards of limited width, some kind of edge-to-edge joint was required. One of the earliest used was the rebate (pronounced "rabbit"), for which see DRAWING 3. It provided an overlap, useful in nailing, and essential when the wood shrank as it dried. The joint might open up a little, but no daylight or draught could come through.

The backs of settles, for example, were often of rebated boarding; and that early and attractive form of sheathing showing the shadow-moulding was usually held together by a rebate concealed among the vertical shadows. We also find a simple bead, or half-round moulding, serving the same purpose of concealing the crack, which it was impossible to eliminate.

An improvement on the rebate, used very early, is the tongue and groove joint, which holds solidly against pressure from either side. It is really an elongated mortise and tenon, and was regularly used to fit wide sheathing edge to edge.

The same in principle, but quite different in effect, is the feather edge joint. Its arrival on the scene marks a turn in fashion from mediæval traditions of cabinet-making to the carefully planned panelling of the Renaissance. One can see from the drawing that it is in effect but a tongue and groove joint, developed a little, both practically and aesthetically. This attractive combination of lines and surfaces was rapidly taken up as the approved way of building up a surface, whether in parallel strips or in the form of panels.

The feathered edge of the board was usually left free to shrink or stretch with the weather, while the beaded edge was nailed to the frame behind it. On vertical boarding the practice varied. Sometimes one board had both its edges bevelled and the next board both edges grooved and beaded; more often, each board had a bevel on one edge and a bead on the other. The writer has seen both methods used on a single wall. Used in connection with panels, the rails and stiles (horizontal and vertical framing pieces) always were grooved to receive a bevelled-edge panel. It is at this point that we touch furniture again; for in the panelling of chests, of cupboard doors, or even of the backs of settles, we find, in all good work, this same use of the bead and the feathered edge or bevel. It is only in much later work that the bead is omitted.

When bevelling does not extend along the whole length of the edge, as of a ceiling beam, or the post of a trestle table, it is called a chamfer, and the decorative way in which it is treated at either end is called a stop. The most familiar stop is the lamb's tongue, which is a curving and tapering transition from the chamfer to the right-angle corner, very easily made. Beyond the stop sometimes the angle is notched once or twice—a detail that we are often asked to believe represents a tally of the Indians disposed of!

With this general knowledge of the principles employed it is hoped that the pieces illustrated in the following pages will not seem strange or complicated.

3. HARDWARE

IN THE FIRST YEARS of the Seventeenth Century, there were two types of hinges used for chests. One was the hardwood dowel, (see DRAWING 4 for Development of Hinges) but more common was the bent wire, or staple hinge. It was made on the link principle, and its ends were driven through the lid and through the back board of the chest and then clinched. For lids, these two hinges were used for a century or more, but for doors, in which the swinging plane was vertical, other forms were required.

If the principle of the link is retained, and the staples made into flat surfaces that can be nailed to door and post, the butterfly hinge (DRAWING 4) is the result. Nails driven through holes in the wings pass through the boarding to be clinched or turned back upon themselves. In the most careful work leather washers were put between the nailheads and the hinge, to keep the door from rattling by taking up any slack that might develop.

The butterfly hinge was excellently suited for use on light and narrow cupboard doors and desk lids. For wider and heavier doors and lids the strap hinge was made, reaching out with its iron arm to get a wider distribution of the nail holes and a better purchase. This hinge can be traced back to the Roman Empire. The strap often hung from a gudgeon or pintail, a vertical finger in the end of a heavy spike driven into the side of the doorway; or it was linked into a wedge, or a half butterfly, or a whole butterfly, or even a graceful sweep of iron, called a buck's horn or a ram's horn, according to its final twist. The strap tapered gracefully and sometimes thinned out, too, as it ran out to the end, which was almost invariably either a simple round like a thumb-mark, or a little flame, usually pointing straight out, sometimes swirling gracefully to one side.

As a matter of fact, this linked joint made probably the most handsome hinge, but there was a more satisfactory solution in the offing. This was the idea of the pinned hinge.

When were these pinned "H"-hinges first manufactured? The writer does not know. However, he has seen photographs of pierced iron pinned "H"-hinges in a French museum publication, catalogued as "XV and XVI Siecles"; and he has seen a very beautiful "H"-hinge described by its English authority as "circa 1525." Furthermore, the following enlightening paragraph appears in a publication of the Victoria and Albert Museum:

"Door hinges of Jacobean (i.e. first quarter of Seventeenth Century) interiors are of the 'H' type, either of twin vertical plates with the ends silhouetted in the outline of eastern domes, or with the same reversed and pierced in the horizontal ends. Generally, however, hinges are of the curving twin 'cock's head' design, but even in such the variations appear endless."

Why, then, are they not immediately the typical interior hinge in America? According to a man who is thoroughly skilled in the craft the probable answer is that the workmanship on them was a little too exacting for the early settler's equipment of tools. If the hinge is to operate efficiently the pin must be quite round, smooth, and carefully fitted. At first this was beyond the powers of the settlers.

Many of the first "H"-hinges to appear in this country were imported from English makers. But before the century was out our own blacksmiths were turning out pin hinges, not only of the strap and butterfly types, but of the "H" and "HL" and "LHL" patterns as well.

The "H"-hinge was forged into the required thickness and bent into the grip required to hold the fixed pin. The edges, as on strap hinges, were hammered to a bevel to cut down the apparent thickness. Variations from the plain "H" included a decorated "H," with ends formed "in the outline of eastern domes"; an "HL," formed by the addition of a strap to run out on the rail of the door and supposed in some quarters, by the mere suggestion of the name of the infernal regions, to have given protection against the evil influence of witches; and very rarely an "LHL," each side having its horizontal strap.

Lastly, we should mention the cockscomb pattern, even though it is very rarely met with here, and quite likely was always imported, as its customary coating of tin suggests. The design is based upon an "H," with each of the four protruding ends curved boastfully and ending in a cock's head facing out. The fact that it was never accepted universally by the American Colonies while having such a popularity in the mother country is perhaps illustrative of a fundamental difference all through the arts. Our work, for many reasons, followed European patterns in simplified forms.

The next and final step is the modern butt hinge. The idea of concealing the plates of the hinge by setting them into the door and its frame was experimented with, first in wrought-iron and brass, just before the Revolution. Then, in 1775, came the English patented invention of cast butt hinges. These new inventions, imported at first, then manufactured here, completely supplanted all other hinges for interiors, once the war was over. On outside doors the use of the strap hinge was long continued, and for barn doors it has never been entirely replaced.

Drawer pulls and escutcheons (the decorative plates protecting the key holes) often are very reliable clues to the age of a piece of furniture. If you are sure that these embellishments were attached at the time the piece was made, you can go a long way toward giving it a correct date. (See Drawing 5 for Developments of Drawer Pulls.)

As the escutcheons usually take their character from the plates that decorate the pull, no mention will be made of them beyond the fact that they are usually slightly larger, though in some instances smaller, than the pairs of handle plates with which they are used, and on which they centre.

The first pulls were of wood, and on account of their size and shape we may call them "thumb-pulls." The pull is plugged into a hole in the drawer-front and secured there either by the tightness of the fit, by a wedge driven from the inside, or by a dowel sunk into it through the top of the drawer-front. These pulls were made of hard wood with the grain running with the axis. Their use continued through the Seventeenth and well into the Eighteenth Centuries. Late Eighteenth and early Nineteenth Century knobs, on the other hand, were flat, like buttons, and were held in place by screws, and the grain ran at right angles to the axis. The typical Nineteenth Century knob is of the same shape, but made in three pieces, a screw of hard wood, a turned head, and a veneered turned cap of mahogany to match the material of the drawer or door.

Brasses first made their appearance in America about 1675. All of the early patterns were cast, and decorated with a primitive symmetrical stamping of circles, arcs of circles, and some straight lines. We notice two changes: there is a steady mechanical improvement, and there is at the same time a change in design, accompanying the change in form of the furniture itself.

The first pull is what is called the drop handle. The drop, cast sometimes a solid round and sometimes but a half round and hollowed out as well, swung from a bent wire which passed through the plate and through a hole in the drawer-front to be spread, like a cotter-pin, on the inside. The wires were sometimes half-circular in section, at other times they were round but hammered flat at the bend to make a neater hold upon the drop. The plate was often a moulded button-like casting, finished in a lathe, but more typically a fancifully scalloped square sheet of very thin brass—often as thin as three sixty-fourths of an inch.

The first mechanical improvement came as the bail handle. It was a crescent of cast brass with the ends turned in and headed much like the modern finish nail. These two ends were held in place by the bent wires that were still the means of fastening. The plate, now spread out to back up the widespread ends of the handle, was usually stamped, but sometimes appeared with a plain surface. Either of these handles is likely to appear as late as 1720, but of the two the drop handle is the earlier.

Sometimes among these bail-handle brasses you find the handle turning outward through the wires instead of inward. This may quite possibly show the transition to the next type, first appearing about 1710, in which the handles, turning outward, are held by little cast screw bolts, hand threaded, and fastened on the inside of the drawer with irregular, hand-made nuts. For a while the tendency was all toward simplification, both of the outline and of the surface decoration. Then the outline grew more complicated again, and through a series of mutations the large elaborate willow brasses were evolved, but with no change in the construction.

These brasses were in fashion until about 1800. Dating from 1770, there appeared the first examples of pressed brass plates, made from sheets as thin as one sixty-fourth of an inch and strengthened by being stamped into decorative designs. They were commonly protected with a coat of lacquer, which may be flaked off to-day with a thumbnail. One common type has the handles turning in again, and in another we see the arrival of the ring handle which was used so frequently by the designers of the Empire period.

Lastly we should mention the little brass handle (in the centre of the bottom row in DRAWING 5) that seems to have worked its way into furniture from its architectural origin. Through the middle of the Eighteenth Century it was used on small iron latches, and is itself perhaps a dapper descendant of the sturdy wrought iron knockers and latch lifters of the previous century. As an adjunct to the cabinet-maker's equipment it was useful on many smaller pieces, such as dressing glasses, writing boxes, tea caddies, and many others.

PLATES

4. WALL BOXES

A WALL BOX, as its name implies, is a receptacle that was designed either to hang from a nail on the wall or to rest against the wall on a table or chest or ledge where it might hold, readily accessible, candles, spices, salt, or whatever else the housewife chose to put in it. In its simplest form, it is merely a box without a lid. Then, as the design is elaborated, a lid is added and drawers appear underneath, first one, then more than one, until finally the well, or main receptacle, is eliminated, and the wall box has become what we may call a wall box of drawers.

From the form of the wall box with drawers there was developed one of the very choicest of colonial furnishings, the pipe box. Into the open box, bowl first, were thrust the long-stemmed churchwarden pipes of clay, or sometimes iron, while a supply of tobacco filled the little drawer beneath. The parts and proportions of the piece became almost as definitely fixed as the features of the human face, and yet no two pipe boxes are alike. Some of them are exceedingly lovely.

It is hard for us to-day, with our kitchen cabinets, ample cupboards, and elaborately built-in shelving, to appreciate how useful these old wall boxes must really have been. But their usefulness is indicated by the way drawers increased in number until the nail would support no more, and boxes of drawers were built to be stood conveniently on other furniture.

It is not intended that what has been here said shall be taken as an exact description of an historical development. That would be difficult to write. The designs are merely considered in order, from the simplest to the most complex. That there may be some chronological correctness to this sequence is suggested by the fact that we do see an analogous evolution of the American chest.

In these boxes the boards have been dovetailed or rebated snugly into one another and secured with an occasional nail, even in the boxes made when nails were available to do all of the work of holding them together. The method of their making had become a fine tradition.

There are, of course, many others, and one is always hoping to discover examples. We shall let one example represent them all, by saying that we look forward to the day when we shall see in the dusty rear of a store of moderate prices a real cocked hat box.

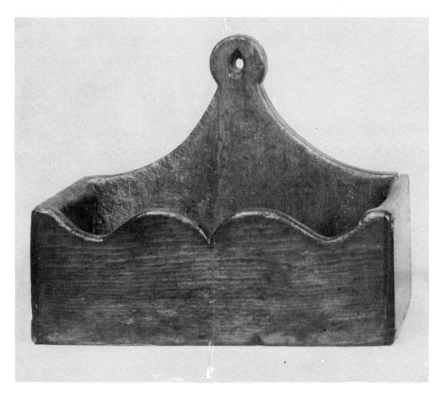

I

A WALL BOX, in its simplest form, probably used to hold candles. Long after the edges and corners had been worn smooth and rounded, the box was rejuvenated with a coat of red paint and a thin yellow striping that encircled the top, following, in a general sort of way, the cupid's bow of the front edge. This painted decoration has lately been removed. [SEE DRAWING 6.]

2

ILLUSTRATING the next type. The candle box is now fitted with a lid, a piece of three quarter inch board constructed with a rebate so that it fits partly into the well. How much less attractive it would have been had the lid shown its full thickness. [SEE DRAWING 7.]

3

WITH the design developing one step further, we find, as happened with the chest, a drawer added beneath the box proper.
This wall box with drawer is owned by the Concord Antiquarian Society. [SEE DRAWING 8.]

4

SOMETIMES several drawers appear beneath the well. But even in the crudest pieces, such as this one, we are apt to find some play of fancy. Here, the knobs increase in size as the drawers grow deeper.

5

A WALL BOX with two shelves. Top and bottom edges of the face boards are moulded with a small thumbnail moulding.

6

AN UNUSUALLY beautiful pipe box. The design at the crown is as crisp as can be, every curve acquiring especial interest either by reversing on itself (on the front) or by running a little beyond 90° (on the back and sides). [SEE DRAWING 9.]

7

ANOTHER pipe box. The tapering proportions were undoubtedly suggested by the long and tapering clay pipes that these boxes were built to hold.

8

THE SCROLL TOP to this two-drawer pipe box would indicate a
date in the middle of the Eighteenth Century. The pipe stems
stick down through the square holes and disappear inside a deep
box, leaving just the bowls showing. Mr. John M. Woolsey is
the owner.

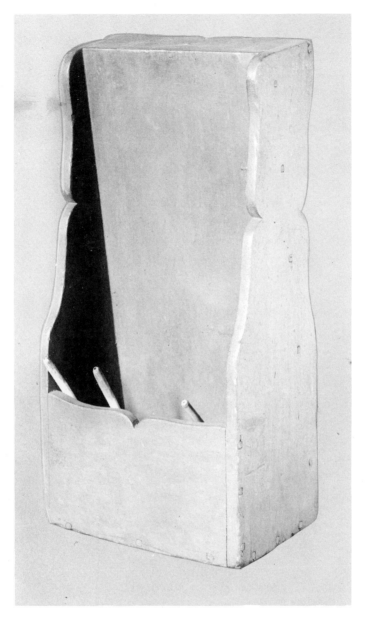

9

THIS LITTLE PIPE BOX is but 15¾ in. high, 5 in. deep, and 7¾ in. wide. It is built of half-inch wood. It is distinctly an exception to the rule upon which the other ninety-nine out of every hundred appear to have been based. It is from the Morgan-Nutting collection at Hartford.

10

QUITE out of the ordinary is this box, presumably built to hold pipes. It is very simply constructed of boards nailed together. Over this frame is patterned the curious design of mouldings and rosettes, all effected from a single strip. For concave rosettes, the moulding mitres in one way, for convex, in the other. The result is that much sought-for combination of variety with unity. Miss Katrina Kipper of Accord, Massachusetts, is the owner. [SEE DRAWING 10.]

I I

THE MODERN short-stemmed pipes fit very conveniently into this particular pipe box. While the drawer for tobacco is of the customary size and proportion, the well is made much lower and shallower than usual. It could have given but scant protection to the brittle and delicate clay stems. Quite likely this box was designed primarily to hold a supply of tapers. The overall dimensions are 3¼ in. by 6 in. by 10¼ in. All of the wood is 5/16 in. thick except the front of the drawer, which is given an extra eighth of an inch for luck.

12

THE BOX at the left is a crude attempt to reproduce, in pine, the tinder box so common in the early days.

The box to the right is an unusually good knife-scouring box. Most of them are so heavily constructed as to rob them of any elegance. In use, the box was taken down from the wall and laid flat on a table. A knife, with its blade on the block and its handle running parallel to the handle of the box, could easily be scoured with a damp cloth or a piece of cork, dipped from time to time in the grit that the box contained. When the process was completed the box was returned to its nail and the grit fell back again into its open well.

13

IT IS HARD to explain why the block of this knife-scouring box slants to the right rather than the left. Perhaps it was built for a left-handed person.

The wooden latch beside it is old and in its original position. Such catches were almost invariably of oak, for the strain upon them would split a softer wood. One can see the latch string leading up and through a hole in the stile of the door. The Colonial hint that corresponded to the report of "not at home" was simply to pull the latch string back through the hole. The property of Mr. F. H. Trumbull of New Boston, New Hampshire.

14

A WALL BOX of drawers. A plaster wall with neither too smooth nor yet too rough a finish to it makes an ideal background for pine and pewter. The property of Mr. Albert H. Atkins, of West Gloucester.

15

THIS is known as a table chest of drawers, from the fact that it is much too small to have stood by itself, even though it is finished in a strong fashion, with generous base and top mouldings. It is dated about 1710, and its origin put down as New England. The drop handle, as is evident even in the photograph, is a restoration, but an intelligent one, for in a piece of as much refinement as this there would quite likely have been just such elaborate pulls. The gradual deepening of the drawers is similar to that in the wall box owned by the writer, and shown as No. 4. In the Morgan-Nutting collection at Hartford.

16

A SET of spice boxes. Such a set was not designed to hang from a wall, but to be set against it on a ledge or table. The set is 18 in. long, 9 in. high, and 7½ in. deep.

17

A PYRAMID of spice drawers. Of course, such drawers as these
may have been used to hold many things other than spices.
"Spice box" is an accepted term nowadays which should be
taken broadly.

18

A MOULDED LID and a pair of scrolled oak braces into which are run the wooden dowels of the hinges—nothing more! This little box, measuring 3¾ in. by 5½ in. by 3¾ in. is in the collection of Mr. Henry W. Erving.

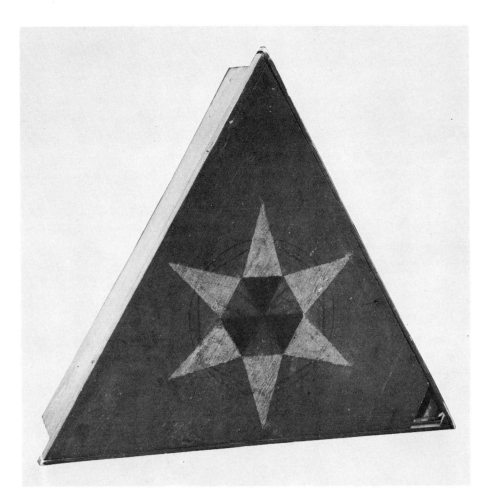

19

IF YOU KNEW that there once were such things as wooden boxes in which the Colonials were accustomed to keep their best cocked hats between festival occasions, there would be no doubt in your mind as to what this box was made for. It is of very light construction, intended to be placed handsomely on top of a chest of drawers, where the decoration would be appreciated and the hat out of harm's way.

This particular box is stained the familiar red, with the star painted in black and in light red-orange. On the back you may read this thrifty New England sentiment:

"February 23, 1786, Stephen Putnam.
Take care of your hats and everything else
if you'd thrive."

The box is to be seen in the Munroe Tavern, the property of the Lexington Historical Society. [SEE DRAWING 11.]

5. CHESTS

THE EARLY AMERICAN HOUSE, in general, must have had relatively little in it that existed solely for decoration. To be sure, we do hear of "carved wooden things," imported from the Indies, which, from their very descriptions, were of use unknown, and there were many pictures on the walls of such thrilling subjects as "one bunch of grapes with a pomegranate." Objects that broke up the bareness of the walls and floor and that hung decoratively by the chimney must each have served some useful purpose, but these pieces were nearly all made with all the refinement that their makers could reasonably give them.

Among the most common of early furnishing was the chest. It was at once a trunk for travel, a place for storage, a bench, and even a table, for at least one chest has been found with checker squares scratched on it.

The earliest pine chests were mere boxes with hinged lids. Some rested flat upon the floor; more often the end boards were carried down and cut into a semblance of legs. As the type developed, drawers were added between the well and the floor—first one, then more, until, in time, the well was inconveniently high, and was given up. The chest with drawers had become a chest of drawers. It only remained for inventive minds to place the whole on an attractive frame and so to make the much prized "highboy." Similarly there evolved the chest on chest, and one wag has proudly proclaimed himself the owner of a chest on chest on floor.

Sometimes, especially in Pennsylvania, chests were decorated with painted designs. Others were scratched lightly with straight and curved line patterns, or were carved on front and ends after one or more of the limited number of conventional designs. Initials, dates, hearts, tulips, sunflowers, scrolled leaves are perhaps the most common of the designs. Mr. Lockwood, in his excellent book, counts ten distinct motifs and shows them to be the basic designs of practically all of the carving done in this country in the early years.

When we try to date definitely a pine chest or some other piece, we immediately run into difficulties. In the first place, there is so little about them that one may technically speak of as style. There were no Hepplewhites or Sheratons guiding the public taste through published designs. It was a much more simple process, not unlike the survival of the fittest, for when an innovation met with the unsolicited approval of the people of the day, it became a common type. Marked changes came slowly, and vestiges lingered long. An elaborate court cupboard might, of course, be mentioned in the inventory of a property, and it might be traceable to-day, back through generation after generation—but a beautifully constructed blanket chest of pine might appear as one of "three chists," or even pass unmentioned.

There are, however, a number of ways of gathering sufficient information to date a piece with a fair degree of accuracy. One should examine the construction. If the boards are not joined together, but are simply nailed one against the other, we should regard the piece suspiciously at once. Probably nothing constructed so poorly would have survived the two hundred years of hard treatment that its lack of quality would have brought down upon it. Nails of the early period were hand-wrought, angular, irregular, roughly flat-headed, and for just these reasons extremely efficient. They were scarce and were used sparingly.

It should be remembered that the very earliest drawers slid on runners in grooves cut in the sides of the drawers themselves. (See Drawing 12.) This made a perfectly working drawer, but it must have seemed unnecessarily awkward to construct, for at a very early date they changed to the typical late Seventeenth Century method of sliding the drawer directly upon its bottom board, which was either flush with or extended over the back and sides, and was rebated into the front. This flush-bottom construction could not have worked as smoothly as was desired, for sometimes we find nailed on this form of bottom two thin strips of wood, one at either side, to act as skids, thus letting the main portion of the drawer run without friction.

The modern solution was then just around the corner. By the end of the Seventeenth Century, the drawer bottom was bevelled and housed into the front and sides, and set just far enough up into the drawer to keep it from touching anything as the drawer slides in and out. The effect is exactly like that of the flush-bottom drawer running on skids, and the construction is much neater.

It was at first the custom to join the sides into the fronts of drawers with a shouldered corner. Dovetailing came into use first at the back edges, then in its more refined form, or lap dovetail, it supplanted the shouldered corner at the front. It may be noted that joints in early work are invariably large and coarse; in later work the proportions are more like those of joints made to-day.

The introduction of a little lip or quarter-round moulding all around the edges of the drawer-front, to hide the inevitable crack, completes the evolution of the modern drawer. This lip appears as early as 1725.

At times, a detail of a piece of furniture suggests a date, itself. The little half-round moulding nailed over the side grain of the wood of the blanket chest shown in Plate 35 is an approach to style and suggests a date between 1690 and 1710. If the moulding shows two smaller half-round reeds instead of the single one, 1710-1720 might be guessed at. (See Plate 38)

If a chest has its original brasses they may tell you a great deal. (See DRAWING 5 and Chapter III.) If the brasses are not original, the fact is usually disclosed by holes or markings on the inside of the drawer-front made by their predecessors. If they are merely reproductions of the earlier types, the brasses have a thickness and a mechanical appearance that are unmistakable. Of the later types a judgment is more difficult, but machine-made threads on the studs and nuts are obvious.

20

HERE is a chest perfectly illustrative of the finest products of the period before pine was generally accepted. The chest is mainly oak, what pine there is having been relegated to secondary positions. Lids, however, were often of pine, because oak was so heavy. The property of Mr. Charles H. Tyler of Boston.

2 1

THE top of this oak and pine chest measures 1 ft. 7½ in. wide by 3 ft. 8¾ in. long, by ¾ in. thick, and is 2 ft., 2½ in. above the floor. The drawer is rebated on the vertical edges and slides on side runners. The frame is oak; the top, all panel boards, and even the mouldings and little triangular blocks on the front, are pine. It is a chest of peculiar interest, showing a step in the transition from the mediæval form of panelling toward the accepted form of the Eighteenth Century. The front is panelled in mediæval fashion. Flat-faced boards are set into rebates in the rails and stiles, the panel thus being recessed about a half an inch from the face of the frame that holds it. A moulding might be set into the angle, or the corners might be cut off, as here, for decorative reasons, but the type is still the old type. The front face is finished relatively smooth to show off either the grain or the carved or painted decoration. But the back of the panel is an irregular affair, often just a rift surface, bevelled on all four edges so that it will fit snugly at the junction with the frame. Thus we get the curious situation of a heavy board, say ¾ in. thick, held on all four sides by a feather-edge as thin as ¼ in., and proving perfectly strong! The structural principle involved is the same as that which permits a carpenter to notch a 10-in. floor joist down to 4 or 5 in. at the ends without appreciably weakening it. The builders were ashamed of the bevel at first, though, and put it always on the inside of the front or sides, or the outside of the back, where it would be the least conspicuous. The change came when they saw the possibilities of a well finished bevel side. Panelling executed an about-face and one more mediæval tradition vanished. The chest shown here has the new form on the ends but the old form on the front. The bevelled panel, held in by a quarter-round moulding, continued as the accepted way of fitting a board into a rail, or one board against another, until well through the Eighteenth Century. This chest is in the collection of the Rhode Island School of Design.

22

THIS CHEST bears a resemblance to the preceding one in that the end panels show a bevel on the exterior, while the central panels are flat. The chest below the lid measures 2 ft., 6 in. high, 4 ft. long, and 1 ft., 7¾ in. wide. The lid and the panels are pine. The drawer is of side runner construction.

Among the other objects shown in the photograph we call attention to the plaster-of-paris deer, painted brown with a white face and yellow horns. From the collection of Mrs. De Witt C. Howe and now in the Currier Art Museum in Manchester, New Hampshire.

23

HALF-ROUND TURNINGS, such as those shown on this chest, were placed there in accordance with a custom that prevailed in the Seventeenth Century across the Atlantic. It was a queer style, for structurally they are of no value whatsoever. One is meant to suppose them to be made of ebony, but underneath the coating of black paint is usually found soft, easily turned whitewood. Oak was used for the frame, and pine for the lid, the panels, and the drawers. The panels are handsomely painted and the drawer-front carved with the owner's initials: "W R E" The chest lid measures 1 ft., 8½ in. by 4 ft., and stands 2 ft., 7½ in. above the floor. On it rests a Bible box, all of pine, even to the carved front board. It is but 6 in. high, 1 ft., 8½ in. long and 11 in. wide. The property of Mr. Henry Ford of Detroit, Michigan.

24

CHESTS of this sort, decorated with conventionalized tulips and sunflowers, are so thoroughly indigenous to the state of Connecticut that they are usually spoken of to-day as Connecticut chests. Such carving abroad would appropriately be called "peasant carving," but in this country it represented quite another thing, for none but the most successful Pilgrims had anything so beautifully constructed.

The half-turnings add tremendously to the effect of the decoration. They were customarily a little less than half a complete circle in section. One ingenious cabinetmaker to-day takes advantage of this fact by the following method. On either side of a thin piece of whitewood he glues a piece of the wood of which he intends to make his spindles. This piece of three-ply he puts on his lathe, turning it to a detail that suits his fancy. Soaking the turning in water separates the three pieces, giving him two spindles slightly less than half round, and a thin pattern of whitewood, which he keeps for reference.

Mr. Charles H. Tyler of Boston is the owner of this chest.

25

ALONG one section of that golden thread, the Connecticut River, a very definite sort of decorated chest, known as the Hadley type, was built in a number of variations. The name "Hadley" is a modern one, originating more or less accidentally as a result of the mention of one of these valuable chests that was found in Hadley, a town in western Massachusetts in the valley of the Connecticut River. But inasmuch as the town thus brought into prominence locates these unique designs fairly accurately the name "Hadley chest" has apparently come to stay. It is a framed chest,with lid, back, and inside boarding of the drawers of pine. The front is carved with a decoration inspired by the tulip tree, but greatly formalized. Flowers, leaves, and stems stand out, the background around them being set back about a sixteenth of an inch, pricked into a rough texture with a pointed stamp, and painted. The foliage is not rounded any further, but some drawing is done, bringing out the leaf ribs and petals by means of incised lines of uniform width, approximately a sixteenth of an inch across.

The Hadley chest shown here is a most perfect example. Little would its original owner, Mary Pease, have believed that more than two centuries after her time the modest carving of her name would be admired daily by several thousand persons as they pass through the chain of old rooms in the Boston Museum of Fine Arts. The sunken carving of the letters of her name is picked out in black paint, and the background and incised lines of the tulip pattern are likewise painted in either red or black, the designer playing the one color against the other, roughly in alternating bands according to the construction of the chest. Around this delicate coloring, the oak and pine appear in the soft mellow texture that the centuries have given them. The property of Mr. Charles H. Tyler of Boston.

26

VERY seldom do we find the lids of chests panelled. Here, both on the lid and on the front a panelled effect is produced entirely by the application of mouldings. The chest, which is 4 ft., 1 in. long and 1 ft., 11 in. wide, was originally painted, red still showing in the panels and a very dark green upon the raised mouldings. The block feet showing here are but pieces of wood placed there to bring the front of the chest up to the height of the sill on which it rests against the wall.

The wall cupboard showing in the centre of the photograph is 6 ft., 5 in. tall, 2 ft. wide, and 1 ft. deep, inside measurements. It projects but $7\frac{1}{4}$ in. from the sheathing, the remainder of the depth coming from its being sunk into the wall the depth of the frame. The lower portion opens as does the upper, both swinging on cotter-pin type hinges.

This is a view of the old kitchen in Mr. Albert H. Atkins's house at West Gloucester.

27

THE DECORATION on this chest may very appropriately be called "line carving." The pattern is really but the patient tracing of a series of lines upon wood by means of a chisel. In the writer's opinion, the term "scratch carving" means nothing at all. If we speak of "scratched decoration" the reference is perfectly clear, and should refer to that decorative treatment effected by the actual scratching of the surface of a board by metal-pointed compasses or by ruled lines. It is usually accompanied by stamped patterns, for the two methods have much in common, being primitive, and by no stretch of the imagination to be considered carving, as no wood is cut away.

This chest measures 2 ft., 9½ in. by 1 ft., 7 in., by 1 ft., 6½ in., and is in the Metropolitan Museum.

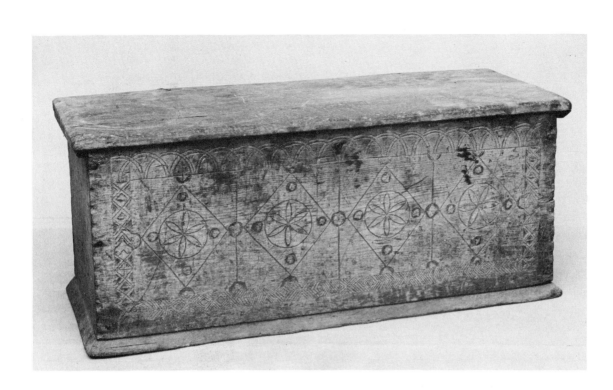

28

THIS CHEST with line carved decoration was found in a barn in Hampton, New Hampshire. The carving is typically that of Seventeenth Century America, for the figures are all geometrical and there is the band of interlacing arches so charactertistic of the later Sixteen Hundreds. The similarity between this chest and that owned by the Metropolitan Museum (Plate 27) is so striking that we know there must have been some connection between the two. Either they were done by the same man, or one was a simplified copy of the other by a less skillful worker. When the writer first discovered the similarity between the designs, he investigated the carving of this chest with great care, fearful lest it might be a recent application to an old chest. His suspicions were unfounded, however, for across the wide checks where the wood in drying had pulled apart, the chiselled lines were broken in perfect consistency, and as the board now stands could never have been cut. This chest was made in an astonishingly casual fashion, for both the interlacing arches and the lozenges had to be compressed naively to make them come out evenly at the end of the run. The "V"-cut line measures about ⅛ in. across. The circles appearing upon the points of the lozenges are sunk, slightly rounded, and stamped with a nail. On the front and top edges there is the familiar notching with, in this case, ¾ in. spacing of the cuts. A thumbnail moulding is faintly visible on both the front and back edges of the lid. To have any moulding at all at the back is unusual. The measurements are 1 ft., 4 in. by 4 ft., 4 in. by 1 ft., 4½ in. high below the lid. The ends are rebated into the front and back. Formerly the lid, 1⅛ in. thick, was braced across the grain at either end and swung on iron strap hinges. The place where once there was a lock became for decades the portal of rats.

29

THE DECORATION of this six-board pine chest, including the date 1673, is composed of individual stamped marks from steel tool dies which were a part of every joiner and carpenter's equipment brought with him from England. The stamping on this initialled and dated chest is unusual, because no less than five separate die tools were used, as well as a small thumbnail gouge. This chest was found in Wethersfield, Connecticut, and now belongs to Mr. William B. Goodwin of Hartford.

30

A SMALL SIX-board chest, just too large to be classified under footstools. It is about 13 in. high. On the front and ends of the lid has been worked a little quarter-round moulding, while on the inside appear the initials "T. F. N." with the "N" done wrong way to, as a skilled, but unsophisticated Huckleberry Finn might well have done it. The lid swings on its original wire hinges and there have been at least three locks installed and broken, probably after the keys had been lost. Chests of this six-board type were made in almost any size, even up to 8 ft. in length. [SEE DRAWING 13.]

3 1

AN UNUSUALLY fine six-board chest. The idea of notching the corners is perhaps borrowed from the finer desk boxes.

The four-post bed is maple and a full six feet high.

In the corner of the room, resting on the diagonal bracing of the frame is the contrivance by which the rope web of the old beds was tightened up, much as we string tennis rackets today.

In Mr. Albert H. Atkins's house in West Gloucester, Massachusetts.

32

SUCH a chest as this can be made the subject of much discussion. The hearts painted on the end and around the corners, the arch and shoulder design painted on the front, and even the flowers themselves, rather suggest a Pennsylvania origin. Its lid dimensions are 1 ft., 11 in. by 4 ft., 2½ in. The back of the chest rests now upon the sill, but formerly there were ball feet matching those in front. In high chests where the grain of the end boards runs up and down, the rear feet are sometimes merely a continuation of the end boards, with ball feet on the front corners only. The property of Mr. Albert H. Atkins.

33

IT SEEMS to be a curious fact that some sorts of furniture can be built agreeably in miniature, while others, if reduced in scale, immediately appear freakish. Small chests of drawers are often very beautiful, as is the one here illustrated. Does not the secret lie in this fact: this chest of drawers, though but a foot and a half high, is still perfectly suited to a useful purpose; and its details, the design having been reduced in size from its more familiar contemporaries, have been consistently simplified? The dimensions, under the lid are: 1 ft., 5½ in. high, 1 ft., 4½ in. long, and 8 in. wide. The property of Mr. Henry W. Erving of Hartford.

34

THE BALL-FOOT CHEST shown here still holds its painting: red on
the top of the lid, greenish black on the mouldings, and red
again on the center panels of the drawers. Elsewhere everything
is a reddish-brown. The drawers are of the flush-bottom construction and slide on side runners. The slots in the sides of the
drawers are ⅝ in. wide at the front but have been worn by friction against the runners to 1⅜ in. wide at the rear. The measurements of the lid, which is 3 ft. above the floor, are 1 ft., 9¼
in. by 3 ft., 4 in. Mrs. Samuel Dale Stevens of North Andover,
Massachusetts, is the owner.

35

WHEN this ball-foot chest with drawer had its set of six drop handles, the effect of its being a three-drawer chest must have been carried out very completely. Of course, the two top "drawers" are really a deep well, reached by raising the top board, with a single drawer below. The chest would date from about the beginning of the Eighteenth Century. Owned by Mrs. Richard T. Fisher of Petersham, Massachusetts. [SEE DRAWING 14.]

36

ONE IS NOT surprised to learn that this chest comes from Connecticut, early in the Eighteenth Century, for Connecticut at that time was in the habit of doing things with a little greater richness than were the other New England states. The chest is entirely of pine with the decoration painted upon it, originally in very gay colours; for it was the custom then, just as it was on the Continent in Gothic times, to use the brightest reds, the most vivid greens, the clearest whites, that were available. The top measures 1 ft., 4½ in. by 2 ft., 5 in., and the lid is 1 ft., 7½ in. from the floor—a small chest for one of this type. It is in the Metropolitan Museum, in the Bolles Collection.

37

ONCE IN A WHILE we find the humble six-board chest construction modified to make a chest of drawers. The legs and the scalloped apron here are common with the prototype, but the piece is given an elaborate cornice and the board ends are trimmed with the single arch moulding, placing the date therefore, between 1690-1710.

The miniature chest of drawers has the absurd stature of 7¼ in. The upper left drawer is constructed with a flush bottom, the upper right and the centre drawer are cut out of single blocks of wood, and the lower drawer is of the latest type, with the bottom rebated and raised. How can one explain all that except by attributing to the maker a very whimsical character indeed? In the collection of Mr. Albert H. Atkins of West Gloucester.

38

THE PRESENCE of two or more drawers beneath the well often
led the maker to carry the draw design all the way up to the top,
as in this instance. The two upper divisions, therefore, are false.
The piece fortunately has all its original brasses, which are of
the type described in the text as being of the second period, in
use not later than 1720. The double reed moulding makes it
probable that the piece dates no earlier than 1710, thus giving
us a fair assurance of 1710-1720 being correct. The owner is Mr.
Samuel Temple of Lynnfield, Massachusetts.

39

IN THIS CHEST the well no longer appears and we have a chest of drawers with fine ball feet balanced by a heavier cornice than would usually have been built had the top been a hinged covering of a well. The double reed moulding was in common use from 1710-1720, and is usually to be found with brasses of this type, which in this instance are a proper restoration. The property of Mr. A. G. Baldwin, of Wakefield.

40

THE CONSTRUCTION of this piece is at once evident and very satisfying. The five drawers are made up in the form of a simple box to which a mitred cornice is applied. The whole then merely sets into the rebate of the solidly joined framework of the base. The owner is Dr. Henry L. F. Locke, of Hartford.

THIS CHEST of drawers on ball feet is black and decorated with a vine pattern that probably once was white, although now it is a dull yellow. The berries at the vine ends are red, and the occasional fanciful wiggles are of the same white, put on evidently with a contrivance that must have resembled a very coarse comb with six or seven teeth. Apparently the decorator's idea was to fill up any particularly blank area with this crude pattern. The double-arch moulding around the drawers, and the flush-bottom construction of the drawers themselves, place the piece in the first quarter of the Eighteenth Century. The owner is Mr. Allen French, of Concord, Massachusetts.

42

IN THIS little chest on frame are shown a most satisfying number of features of the earliest construction. The frame is oak, posts from 2 in. square, and stretchers from 1½ in. square, in what is known as "ball" turning. The wood of the panels and of the drawer is pine. The drawer-front meets the side pieces in a shouldered corner, and the bottom is flush with the sides, which are themselves grooved and hang on side runners. Dimensions below the lid are 1 ft., 6 in. wide, 2 ft., 2 in. long, and 2 ft., 6½ in. high.

On the chest is a two-light candle holder, 11 in. high, made of hard wood with the centre post ⅞ in. round and threaded to make ten complete turns every three inches. Above hangs a set of pine shelves 1 ft., 8½ in. wide, 2 ft., 6½ in. high, with the three shelves 6 in., 5¼ in., and 4½ in. deep. The wood is ½ in. thick throughout.

Owned by Mrs. De Witt C. Howe, of Manchester, N. H.

43

IT IS interesting to note that frequently there are border line examples that might be placed with equal appropriateness in either of two groups. Here, for instance, is what is listed, in the Morgan Memorial Museum at Hartford, as a chest on frame. So it most certainly is. Yet might we not quite suitably show it in the group of desks, calling it a desk box on frame? The upper portion is a very fair counterpart of the box owned by the writer and shown in Plate 102. The box is made of pine, while the base, as one should expect, is of a hard wood, in this case oak. It is dated, on the label in the Morgan-Nutting Collection, about 1690.

44

ANOTHER PAINTED CHEST is this one with a drawer and set up on a frame. It dates from the end of the Seventeenth Century, is chiefly pine, and is painted in the same general coloring as the one in Plate 36. The background is black, with yellow stems and initials, the flowers and some of the leaves are red.

The top, 3 ft. from the floor, measures 1 ft., 6 in. by 2 ft., 6 in. In the Bolles Collection at the Metropolitan Museum.

45

A PAINTED CHEST of drawers on frame. The date of 1690-1710, which is indicated by the single arch moulding, is somewhat substantiated by the drawing of the little houses, which show casement windows with diamond panes. The double-hung window came into use just after the turn of the century. Among the many interesting and useful stunts that photography can do to-day is that of "holding back" certain colors by the judicious use of filters. In this way the photographer was able here to bring out the painted scenes and scrolls so that they are considerably plainer in the picture than one sees them on the chest to-day. We show the chest here, therefore, more nearly as it appeared two hundred years ago. It is in the collection made by the late Mr. Samuel Dale Stevens, of North Andover, Massachusetts. [SEE DRAWING 15.]

46

THE SINGLE ARCH MOULDING of this painted pine highboy, the drop handles, and the early turnings have led to the assigning of the date of 1690-1700 to this piece. The background is painted black, to set off the birds and flowers, and even bridges, painted in reds and yellows and occasionally greens. The top measures 1 ft., 9 in. by 3 ft., 1 in., and is 4 ft., 4 in. above the floor. In the Metropolitan Museum.

47

THIS HIGH CHEST of pine with double arch moulding and false drawers covering the front of the well shows plainly how difficult it is to say definitely that one piece of furniture is earlier or later than another. We know that the double arch moulding is later than the single, yet we also know that high chests with drawers beneath them eventually were supplanted by high chests of drawers, running way up to the top. Mr. Charles H. Tyler is the owner.

THIS VERY BEAUTIFUL HIGHBOY is of pine, and apparently has never been painted. It may be dated about 1700. It is owned by Mr. Malcolm A. Norton of West Hartford, and is loaned by him to the Morgan Memorial Museum.

IN A FEW rare instances one runs across furniture that has never been painted, never been restored, never lost any of its brasses, never been out of the hands of the descendants of its original owners. Mr. Oliver E. Williams was so fortunate as to procure just such a piece in this pine and maple highboy, which had been for about an even two hundred years in the western part of Connecticut. The drawers are outlined by the familiar double arch moulding which in this case measures 9/16 in. in width and 3/32 in. in thickness. The measurements at the top are 1 ft., 9 in. by 2 ft., 11 in., by 5 ft., 3 in. high. The drawers grade in height, from the topmost and smallest, as follows: 5¼ in., 6⅛ in., 7 in., 8 in., and 8¼ in. It will be seen that this roughly follows the custom mentioned elsewhere in this book of increasing each new drawer by the thickness of the strip of wood between.

At the left of the photograph is a candle stand of the type sometimes supposed to have been used by weavers; at the right is a floor candle holder with sockets for two candles.

50

A PINE HIGHBOY with a scroll top, representing about the last step in the evolution of the chest. The wood is pine throughout, with the exception of the three top finials and the base with ball and claw feet, which are cherry. It is very unusual to find as elaborate a piece as this made in the unsophisticated pine. It is owned by Mr. Robert P. Butler of Hartford.

6. STOOLS AND BENCHES

WHEN WE CONSIDER the destructive treatment to which a footstool is subject, together with the great number to be seen in the shops, homes, and museums to-day, we can get some idea of the quantities that must have been in existence. Of a wide variety of designs, that of four legs thrust into a bored top is the simplest. One might argue that that honour belonged to a structure of just three pieces, as that shown in PLATE 52. There is no bracing, and there are no nails; the scalloped legs are merely tenoned into the top and tightly wedged from above.

To make a more solid structure, sides were added; these were usually cut partly into the legs and nailed in place. These side boards were occasionally curved in pleasing lines.

Another way of bracing the stool longitudinally was to have a board on edge running along the axis of the top, piercing the end boards, and sometimes fixed with wedges. Still another and cruder method was to place braces diagonally from the legs to the underside of the top.

Mention should be made here of the joined stool, for although its frame, like that of a tavern table, was invariably of hardwood, the top was usually of pine. These joined stools were used instead of chairs until the later years of the Seventeenth Century, and American examples are rare to-day.

Footstools were seldom made over eight inches in height, but benches may be considered with them, for they presented the same problem in design, except for the greater strength required. These benches were used as were the joined stools: placed beside the trestle table at meal time, stood in front of the great fireplace, or pushed up against the wall where they would be out of the way.

To make for real comfort, a bench might be provided with a back and ends and even a narrow strip across the top. Such a bench, or settle, stood customarily near the fire, and was drawn before it or swung to one side according to the temperature of the otherwise unheated room.

The plainer settles had nicely outlined end boards, cut into graceful arm rests or, occasionally, drawn up into flat knobs. The more elaborate ones had panelled backs and stronger construction throughout.

It must have been the great size of a settle that led some inventive person to think of a double use for the piece. Of course, the huge well beneath the hinged seat most frequently held wood for the fire, but we sometimes find this space opening out to form a deep bed. It certainly could have been no more uncomfortable than the floor on which it rested, and its eighteen-inch sides effectively kept out the cold draughts that whistled to each other from all low corners of the room.

Another type, designed with the same motive, economy of space, is the settle table, similar to the hutch table, and designed to let the back of the settle swing down to form a table top.

Pine proved to be well suited for use in the footstool and bench because it was the lightest of wood, and pieces made of it were readily moved about.

The limitations of pine are very clearly shown when we come to consider chairs. It was an interesting evolution, including Wainscot chairs, Brewsters, Carvers, slat-backs, banister-backs, Windsors, and the exquisitely designed and constructed chairs after the designs of Chippendale, Hepplewhite, and Sheraton—but almost none were made of pine. The strain to which a chair is subjected could not be taken care of by a soft wood—not that the legs would give under the downward pressure, rather that they would work annoyingly loose about the mortises. An additional point, that turning was not often done in pine, has often been mentioned.

There is one part of a chair for which pine was found to be satisfactory. For a chair seat pine was light in weight, easily shaped, and not easily splintered. In chairs of the Brewster and Carver types pine seats are exceptional examples, while in the Windsors a pine seat is the rule.

It is nevertheless surprising that chairs of pine construction, so frequently made for the use of children, were almost never, it seems, made for adults. This is all the more puzzling when we consider how often settles, both large and small, were made of it.

5 1

ALTHOUGH the scheme of this footstool is simple to the extreme, it is carried out with a very nice detail. The octagonal section of the legs, their taper, their spread toward the floor, and the angle put on the sides of the top all show an appreciation of the difference between grace and clumsiness. [SEE DRAWING 16.]

52

THIS AMUSING little footstool is a model of construction. Wooden wedges have been driven into saw-cuts in the tenons of the legs, as the photograph shows, and so the three boards have held together for perhaps two centuries. Except on the top, where it has worn off, the red paint, daubed with streaks of black, is still showing.

53

OF MUCH MORE usual construction is this five-board stool. If we added a bottom we should have that starting point for so much early construction, the six board chest. (See Plate 30.) Sometimes we find stools of this same design stretched out to a length of 3 ft. or so, to meet the demands of a settle's worth of weary feet. [SEE DRAWING 17.]

54

BOTH LEGS and side pieces of these stools may be found in a great variety of patterns. Extending the sides to act as brackets under the overhanging top is an ingenious scheme often made use of. The black daubing over a red base shows plainly in this photograph.

55

AN ODD adaptation of the five-board type is this fiddle-back
stool belonging to Mrs. Parker Whittemore, of West Gloucester.

56

IT IS a shame that this carefully worked out stool should have broken at the corners because of the very minuteness with which it was put together. It is like a pencil that has broken because it was sharpened to too fine a point. The centre brace is unusual in a small stool.

57

THIS STOOL is unique in having the apron running around all four sides. The designer was evidently getting all the amusement he could out of the Gothic Ogee, or reverse curve, for it appears not only in the legs, as is often the case, but also on each of the four pieces of the apron. [SEE DRAWING 18.]

58

IT IS NOT uncommon for the legs of stools to be slanted outward at the bottom, to give greater stability, as in this example. The stool is painted black, with a red stripe, and although such coloring probably was not originally there, it is handsome enough to save it from the paint remover. The brass pull is a more modern embellishment. The property of Mr. Franklin H. Trumbull, of Concord, Massachusetts. [SEE DRAWING 19.]

59

THIS THREE-LEGGED stool is all of pine and astonishingly light. The top board of the seat is 10¾ in. in diameter and 2 ft., 2 in. above the floor. This rests on a piece 7¾ in. in diameter and 1⅛ in. thick, into which the three legs are secured. These legs are bevelled from 1¼ in. square, and spread until they form an equilateral triangle 22 in. on a side at the floor. The horizontal braces are 1⅞ in. by ⅜ in. and a little over 18 in. long. Owned by Mr. E. Gordon Parker of Cambridge.

60

JOINED or joint stools, so common in the Seventeenth Century, were for two hundred years pushed aside by high back chairs. It is no wonder, therefore, that they are scarce to-day. The Pilgrim father, however, leaning back in his armchair, looked down between the opposing rows of his family, all of them perched as comfortably as might be on forms or stools. No one sat opposite him. Mr. William B. Goodwin has in his house in Hartford a long table, one of the end stretchers of which is worn almost flat where the head of the family rested his feet at mealtime. The opposite stretcher, likewise original, shows no wear at all. As joint stools were commonly used in England it is often difficult to tell an American piece from a European one. The two rules, namely, (1) in England the seats were made of oak while in America they were of pine, and (2) English oak is dark, American oak light in color, are valuable but not conclusive evidence, as the writer has a stool with a top of light coloured oak! The top of this stool is made of 1 in. pine and the legs turned from 2 in. maple, splaying (i.e. spreading) two ways. Examples are found with legs spreading two ways, one way, or not at all. It is owned by Mr. Sellers McKee, of New York City. He purchased it on Long Island at a place where it seemed probable that it had crossed the Sound from Connecticut. [SEE DRAWING 20.]

61

WE INCLUDE this photograph in order to give a picture of a joint stool in its Pilgrim setting. It is difficult for us nowadays to think of a stool as ever having been a first rate member of the furniture family. Yet during the first years of the New England settlements chairs with backs were rarities, reserved for the heads of the families. 'Ware lest you leaned back before you had attained the dignity of that seniority! The setting here is from the Brown-Pearl House, originally in West Boxford, Massachusetts, now set up in the Boston Museum of Fine Arts. It is thoroughly typical of the Seventeenth Century—the "mediæval" period of American architecture and furniture.

62

A JOINED FORM, or bench, standing before one of the seven-foot fireplaces in Mr. Atkins's house at West Gloucester. Such forms were placed alongside the great trestle tables at meal times and most of the family ate in this uncomfortable close-order formation; for the dignity of a chair was for long reserved for the head of the household. This form is 1 ft., 5 in. high. Its top, overhanging 10¾ in. at each end, is 8½ in. wide, 6 ft., 6 in. long, and 1¼ in. thick. The ends are likewise 1¼ in. thick, but the centre brace must have come from another board, for it measures 1½ in. by 1½ in. The wedges that secure the centre brace at either end are easily discovered, and the joining of the legs and the top may be seen, too, if one compares the illustration with Plate 52, which shows a similar construction.

63

THE WAY in which this bench, or form, is fitted together without the use of nails or pegs is quite astounding. The solution of the problem is to be found in the drawing herewith. Owned by Miss Katrina Kipper, of Accord. [SEE DRAWING 21.]

64

OF SLIGHTLY different construction, this form is owned by Mr. A. G. Baldini of Wakefield. [SEE DRAWING 22.]

65

THE SETTLE owned by the Metropolitan Museum and exhibited
in the American Wing, is illustrated here. Like most settles, this
one shows the red stain that was so common, and has no decoration beyond the graceful curving of the side pieces. Occasionally the settle is found with the back curved in a segment of a
circle, with the result that two people sitting beside one another
are turned so that they are slightly facing. The boarding in that
case, of course, is vertical. [SEE DRAWING 23.]

66

ONE OFTEN hears that the little rest between two persons on a settle was intended for a candle. Quite likely. It is the writer's guess, however, that they were more often used as in this photograph. This beautiful settle is in the Shaker Room of Mrs. John C. Spring at West Gloucester, Mass.

67

THIS SETTLE, shown before the old Barker House fireplace after the removal of the latter to Mr. Henry D. Sleeper's house at East Gloucester, came from Marlboro, Massachusetts. It measures 4 ft., 6 in. high and 5 ft., 3 in. wide, curving with a radius of 10 ft., 8 in. The seat is 1 ft., 3 in. deep, and the same height above the floor. The wood is ¾ in. thick, throughout, with the back boards running vertically and joined with a beaded tongue and groove.

Hanging at the right of the fireplace opening can be seen a little heart-shaped piece of pine. It is a box, meant, quite likely, for just the use to which it is put here, holding a spray of everlasting. It is constructed of two boards, one 1 in. thick and hollowed out to make the box, the other ¼ in. thick and used simply as a cover, or front. The total width is 5 in. and the height 8 in.

68

THIS VERY beautiful panelled settle (1700-1750) is built entirely of pine, and was once stained or painted red. The seat tenons into the side pieces—an unusual feature—while the sawn profiles on the armrests and on the projecting front of the seat show an elaboration quite in keeping with the more elaborate panelled construction. The back measures 6 ft., 2 in. long by 4 ft., 6 in. high; the seat is 1 ft., 6½ in. deep and 1 ft., 3 in. above the floor; the wood is 1 in. thick throughout. In the collection of the Rhode Island School of Design.

69

WHETHER or not settle beds were ever in much use in this country, it is hard to say. In general, we think of them as being used by the French Canadians, yet without a doubt there must have been some in the northern parts of Vermont, Maine, and New Hampshire. The two hooks shown in the photograph could be released to allow the top and front boards to swing toward one, opening up what must have been a thoroughly uncomfortable box for one's night quarters. This particular settle bed belongs to Mr. I. Sack of Boston.

THIS IS A CHAIR TABLE, a little too narrow from front to back to be very comfortable as a chair, but a very perfect table which can be set against the wall, as here, when its table properties are not required. It is owned by Mr. I. Sack, and is in the back room of the King Hooper House at Marblehead, Massachusetts, where there is a collection of just the sort of material that this book is being written about. [SEE DRAWING 24.]

THIS SETTLE TABLE is owned by Mrs. Parker Whittemore. She has it in her "Village Green Shop" at Ipswich, Massachusetts, where it is in thoroughly congenial surroundings.

WHEN A CHAIR TABLE of this sort included, among its several parts, a box beneath the hinged lid of the seat, it is usually spoken of as a hutch table. The grace of this design speaks for itself. The top is ⅞ in. thick and 3 ft., 6 in. in diameter. When tipped down, it rests 2 ft., 3½ in. from the floor. The braces running across it are from 1⅜ in. stock, 3 in. wide; the side boards are 1 in. thick and 1 ft., 3 in. wide; the feet are 2½ in. high, 2½ in. wide, and 1 ft., 7½ in. long. All other wood is ⅞ in. thick. The seat is 1 ft., 11½ in. above the floor. Blue paint still covers all of the table except the top, which is quite without colouring above and considerably stained with red on its conspicuous under side. It may be seen in the Morgan Museum at Hartford, to which it has been lent by Mrs. Charlotte R. G. Hanna.

73

THIS CHAIR TABLE is obviously smaller and more delicately fashioned than the previous chair. The long tenons extending through the arm mortices are a curious feature. Owned by Mrs. Parker Whittemore, of West Gloucester.

74

THIS IS A child's chair, the seat being but 3¾ in. above the floor!
The problem was similar to that of the settle, and the solutions
are really quite the same. [SEE DRAWING 25.]

75

IN THE GARRET of the King Hooper House at Marblehead, Mr.
Sack has allotted a corner to children's things. One will appreciate the minute scale when he knows that the bed is just 3 ft.
long and 18 in. wide. The dolls, of course, tend to make the
pieces look larger than they really are.

76

IT IS rather a mystery why so few full-size chairs are to be found built like the settles. Childrens' chairs of this sort exist aplenty, but in the larger sizes they are very, very rare.

This extraordinary example is not as uncomfortable as it looks, nor is it as dangerous to rock in! Under the seat, as is the rule in the few chairs of this sort that the writer has happened to see, is a drawer, accessible from the rear. Owned by Miss Katrina Kipper.

7. STANDS AND TABLES

THE EARLY PURITAN HOUSEHOLD sat down to meals, as had been the custom in England, on one or both sides of a long table. It was usually so large and occupied so much space that, once the meal was over, the removable top was stood up against the wall and the framework or trestles were also moved out of the way. The name "table" was not frequently used at first; we heard of "bords" or "table bords," and so for a long time we find these pieces of furniture so mentioned, even occasionally in the Eighteenth Century.

The frames of these first great table bords were made of oak and the boards themselves were always made of pine, for no great strength was required and pine was light and procurable in pieces of great width. Eventually, there came into common use the "standing" and "dormant" tables already existing on the other side of the Atlantic. They were joined tables with fixed tops, not intended to disappear from sight after the meal was finished. To accommodate a number of guests, ingenious joiners devised "drawing tables," the ends of which pulled out until the length of the table was nearly doubled. These compared favourably in size with the "table bords," for representatives of both may be seen that measure about three feet by twelve feet.

But the drawing table was too complicated to last long, and by the end of the Seventeenth Century it had been superseded by the gate-leg table. Although of fairly simple construction, the gate-leg table could be opened to an amazingly large area, (Lyon mentions one in Edinburgh that is over twelve feet long) and its leaves could easily be dropped, to reduce very considerably the size, when desired. The gate-leg table has always been held in great favour.

The frames of all these tables were always made of the harder woods, but the tops were usually made of pine. Structural strength is not one of the assets of white pine, and tables with turned legs of pine are rare. A table leg, cut into by four mortices, two in the top and two where the stretchers join it, and turned, in places, to small diameters, is not as strong as it appears to be. The choice lay between using a light wood in a heavy framework, or turning a hard, strong wood more delicately. When we run across a table made entirely of pine, we admire the soft quality that time has given to its legs and stretchers, but there is a feeling of wonder that any of the projecting flanges are left at all.

It seems that toward the close of the Seventeenth Century there was a tendency away from the idea of having one big dining table. Tables had many uses other than just that of dining service, so the emphasis shifted from one large table to many smaller ones.

Among the smaller tables were those of the type now known as the tavern table. It consisted of a joined frame of four (or sometimes three) legs, almost invariably turned, connected just above the feet by a circuit of stretchers, or a medial stretcher running between two end ones, either turned or plain. The top was usually rectangular, sometimes round, half-round, or elliptical. There was a single drawer beneath the top. Usually the legs stood vertically on the floor, but sometimes they slanted in. This leads us toward another type, perhaps the most beautiful of all.

With many tables in use throughout a house, as there were toward the close of the Seventeenth Century, one that could be folded or reduced in size in one way or another when not in use must have been particularly desirable. To satisfy this need, several distinct types were evolved. The one that achieved the most delightful combination of sound structure and graceful appearance is known as the butterfly table. This table combined the drop-leaf advantages of the gate-leg table with the simple frame of the slant-legged tavern table. The drop leaves were supported by swinging braces suggestive of wings.

There were other kinds of drop-leaf and folding tables in current use, most notable of which was the "folding" table, two of whose legs swung flat with the other two while the top broke and dropped vertically to the sides. In this form it was nearly as flat as a modern card table when collapsed, and could thus be kept out of the way yet near at hand.

Another type that did its best to flatten itself against the wall is the chair table. Its top is constructed to tip up and form a back to a rather uncomfortable chair. When there was a little box under the seat of the chair, the piece was known as a hutch table.

We should not fail to speak of the many little stands that were quite in fashion. We commonly group them under the one heading of candle stands, but their real uses must have been far more varied than our modern name for them suggests.

The first touch of those styles which, from the point of view of this book, we may call "later," is to be seen in the cabriole leg. Close upon that came the cabinetmakers with their more elegant designs and their different materials. Theirs is another story.

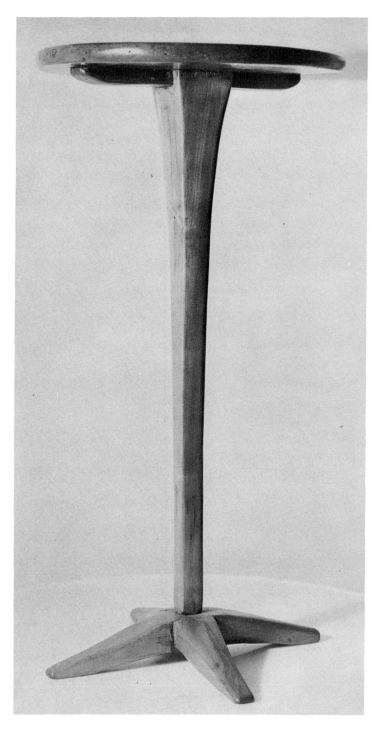

77

ONE RARELY sees as graceful a candle stand as this one, with its tapering stem and claw foot. Structurally, too, it is thoroughly satisfying. It belongs to Mrs. De Forest Danielson, of Boston. [SEE DRAWING 26.]

78

A MAPLE CANDLE STAND with pine top. The top is 1 ft., 1½ in. in diameter and beaded on the edge. The brace, running across the grain of the top is halved into the main post (chamfered to an octagon from 1¾ in. square), which in turn projects into the feet with a ⅞ in. round dowel. The feet are 12¾ in. by 2 in. by 2½ in. high. Miss Katrina Kipper, of Accord, Massachusetts, is the owner.

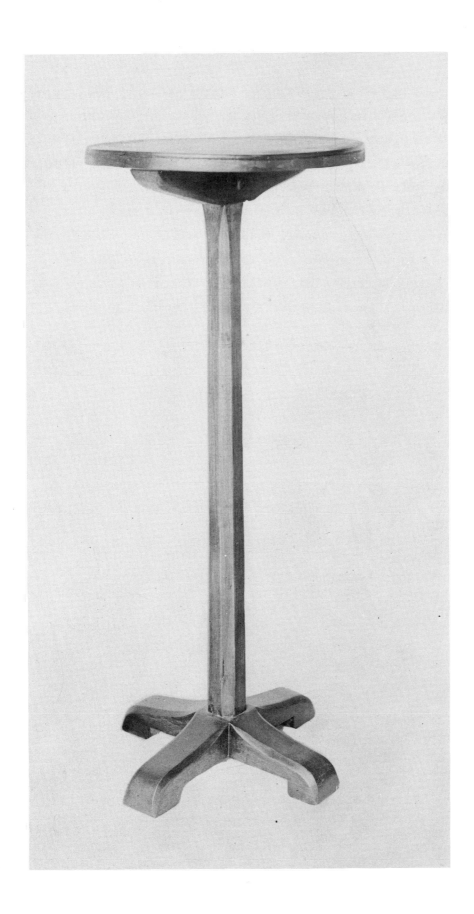

79

THE WRITER was tempted, with the permission of Mr. Charles Andrews, of Boston, who owned it at that time, to make a copy of this chamfered candle stand. In fact, he made two stands with the sparkling decoration on the posts. But in the first experiment he ran the post up an even size from the feet to top, and in the second he tapered the post very accurately from a fairly large top to a fairly small base, and neither table has the vitality of the original. This one seems to have a great deal of the organic feeling that is in Gothic work. It has nubby roots and a flexible stem, with the top bursting like a flower.

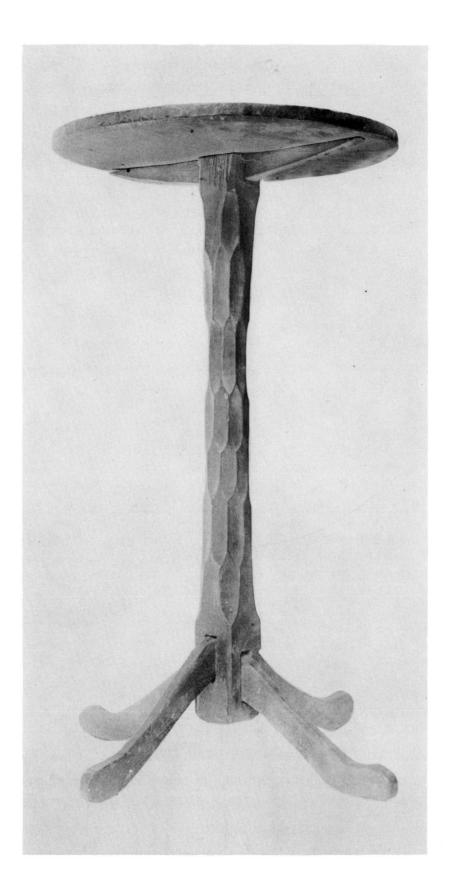

80

A MOST PERFECT weaver's stand of maple and pine. The theory, rather difficult to prove, is that the weaver kept her candle on the stand, which was turned with the crossbar of the "T"-base toward her. She could then pass to and fro at her work with no danger of tripping. At the Wayside Inn, Sudbury, Massachusetts.

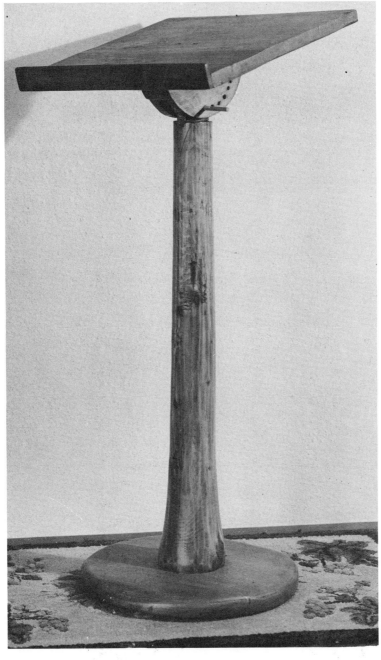

8 1

THE BEST GUESS that we can make for the use of this pivot top
reading stand is that it was made to hold a Bible. The height
of 2 ft., 9 in. precludes the possibility of its being used except by
one who sat before it. The shaft tapers from 4 in. to 2 ¼ in. in
diameter. It is in Mrs. John C. Spring's collection, among the
Shaker pieces.

82

THIS TABLE is the noblest of them all. Others may be more beautiful, or more delicate, or may have had George Washington more frequently to dinner, but this table has a grandeur that is as yet unrivalled. The top is a single plank of pine, 2 in. thick, 2 ft. wide, and 12 ft. long. It is gouged and scratched and, in places, carved, and shows a sprinkling of worm holes; but such markings, like the lines in a fine old face, only increase your reverence for it. The lengthwise brace, or stretcher, is also of pine; all else is oak. The top is in no wise attached to the trestles, for the table was intended to be easily taken apart when room was needed for other purposes. It is hard to believe, however, that the wedges at the three trestles were removed and the frame taken apart three times a day. In the Metropolitan Museum. [SEE DRAWING 27.]

83

TRESTLE TABLES distinctly made at home, like this one, are quite impossible to date. As the top is not attached to the trestles, and as there is no longitudinal stretcher, this sort of table may be set up or taken down in less time than it takes to write about it. The property of Mr. E. Gordon Parker, of Cambridge, who found it in use in a dairy in New Hampshire. [SEE DRAWING 28.]

84

FOR A SMALL "X"-TRESTLE TABLE this is a very fine one. Its usefulness, however, is somewhat limited by its height of only 2 ft.
The photograph shows the top to be cracked. Such is quite apt
to be the case if, in fixing up an old table top, the "bread-board"
strips across the ends are fastened on too rigidly. In the dry air
of a modern house, when the wood wants to shrink, the end
strips must allow it to do so. It can shrink and swell if you have
cut a slot rather than a hole in the strip and have screwed the
strip to the top. A plug of wood can cover the mechanics. This
table, like so many really old examples, is almost too low to be
of general use to-day. Often the explanation is that the turned
feet have first broken and then been sawed off to level the table
again. This particular table, however, never had any section
that could be called a foot, so we must conclude that this is approximately its original height. [SEE DRAWING 29.]

THIS "X"-TRESTLE TABLE is a splendid example. The construction is evident, and the important measurements are: top, ¾ in. by 22 in. by 29 in.; top braces, ⅞ in. by 1⅜ in.; legs, ⅞ in. by 3⅜ in.; centre braces, ⅞ in. by 4½ in.; stretchers, ⅞ in. by 1½ in. Occasionally there is a bottom inserted between the two centre braces, making a convenient place for the storage of knives, forks, spoons, and so on. More often, though, the space is open, as it is in this example. Owned by Mr. Charles Woolsey Lyon, of New York.

86

HERE is the same type of table built in bigger, heavier proportions. The top is ⅞ in. by 2 ft. 7 in. by 7 ft. 2 in., and 2 ft., 4 in. above the floor. It is braced across the grain by a 1½ in. by 2½ in. board above each trestle; the legs are 3 in. by 3½ in.; the centre braces 1 in. by 8 in.; and the stretchers 1 in. by 4 in. Mr. I. Sack, of Boston, is the owner.

87

THE TITLE, split gate-leg, describes this type of table concisely. The leg of the gate, when folded, fits against its neighbour and the split is scarcely noticeable. It is all of hard pine, painted a rich red that comes off a thick paste under the action of a remover. Its past history will probably always be a mystery, for it was purchased in Boston from a peddler right off his wagon. We call attention to the shouldered corner post of the room. It was the custom in Seventeenth Century building to use here an inverted tree trunk. The larger part of the tree, where it swelled out at the roots, was put at the top to give better bearing for the several timbers that had to rest upon it. [SEE DRAWING 30.]

88

THE FRAME of this Seventeenth Century gate-leg table is hard pine, and still in excellent condition, showing that this form of pine can endure as well as oak and maple, although people were reluctant in the early years of the century to use it. The top is ¾ in. soft pine, 2 ft., 2 in. above the floor, and opens to a surface 3 ft., 11½ in. by 4 ft., 1 in., the last dimension being reduced to 1 ft., 6¼ in. when the leaves are down. The frame measures 1 ft., 1 in. by 2 ft., 9½ in. and is made of 2¼ in. square legs and beaded stretchers, and a 1⅛ in. by 5¼ in. beaded apron. The gates are 1 ft., 6¼ in. wide. The owner is Mr. Oliver E. Williams of Boston.

89

THIS TRESTLE GATE-LEG TABLE dates from the last quarter of the
Seventeenth Century. It may be seen in the American Room at
the Metropolitan Museum, to which it is loaned by Mr. Earle
W. Sargent of Asheville, North Carolina. [SEE DRAWING 31.]

90

THIS convenient piece may be designated by the term Tuck-away Gate-Leg Table, for it can be completely flattened when its services are for the time being not required. The top only is of pine. It is the property of the Boston Museum of Fine Arts, where it may be seen in the appropriate setting of the room of panelling from Essex County, Massachusetts.

9I

TRESTLE-FOOT GATE-LEG TABLES are as rare as they are ingenious. As the centre fixed leaf of the pine top is but 5 in. wide and the trestle feet but 10 in., the table folds exceedingly flat when it is put against the wall. Opened up, the top ellipse is 28½ in. by 30 in. and 24 in. above the floor. The legs and stretchers are turned from 1¾ in. maple. The gates swing on pins above and below, running into the rails. Mrs. John C. Spring is the owner.

92

IT IS very seldom that one finds a tavern table with turned legs
entirely of pine. It was usually considered unwise to use a soft
wood when there were going to be delicate flanges in the turnings. The flanges were considered too likely to be broken off.
But when you do come across one like this, it is certainly a find.
Surprisingly light weight, beautifully soft in texture, it is quite
out of the ordinary. The turned feet, which were invariably a
part of the tavern table leg, have gone to pieces and have been
cut off, lowering the 1 ft., 11 in. by 2 ft., 8 in. table to 21 in. high.
The appeal of "Money wanted" is on a church plate of Pennsylvania slip ware.
The property of Mr. Albert H. Atkins, of West Gloucester. [SEE
DRAWING 32.]

93

WE HAVE here another tavern table constructed entirely of pine. One marvels at the lightness. This particular table shows very odd turnings that might be really early. On the other hand, the knobs, which apparently are the original pulls, and the construction of the drawer, show the piece to be comparatively late. Furthermore, no piece of soft pine would be likely to have its feet intact if it had come down from the Seventeenth Century.

94

TAVERN TABLES are sometimes found in lengths that make them suitable nowadays to occupy the central space in a living-room. Usually, of course, they have to serve as side tables. This is Mrs. De Witt C. Howe's living-room at Hopkinton, New Hampshire.

95

WHEN there is a little well or chest beneath the top of a table, it is known as a hutch table. The reason for tipping the tops of these tables was, of course, to permit them to be backed against the wall and out of the way when they were not in use. And that they might not stand idle, the chair and the hutch functions were often included.

The child's rocker is of pine, but, curiously, the spoon rack is of quartered oak.

The property of Mrs. Parker Whittemore, the Village Green, Ipswich, Massachusetts.

96

THIS is a trestle-foot hutch table of poor but honest parentage—for not a moulding plane has been used upon it. The sunk panels, nicely constructed, are held in place by a bevelled stick where certainly a moulding would have been run had there been a suitable plane available. The box beneath the seat is very shallow, most of the space having been given to the drawer. The frame is maple but all wide boards are pine. The ¾ in. top measures 3 ft., 9½ in. in diameter, and when in its table position is 2 ft., 4 in. above the floor.

THIS is the chair table that was shown as No. 73. On top of it is a pine Bible rest that probably attended a great many family prayers in its younger days. Mrs. Parker Whittemore, of Ipswich, Massachusetts, is the owner.

THIS HALF-ROUND TABLE is entirely of pine. It is 2 ft., 2 in. high, 2 ft., 5 in. in diameter, and the three legs with chamfered corners are from 1½ in. square. The fact that table legs of this sort are customarily of pine makes the writer believe that the colonists were less wary of morticing and tenoning pine than of turning it.

The eleven iron pans were used in cooking.

In the corner of the room, with the long and crooked handle, is a whimple, an ingenious device with which the great iron kettle hanging over the fire could be tipped and its contents drawn upon.

Two wrought iron candle holders are shown spiked into the door jamb, one on either side. There must have been a few conveniently placed holes and the lights shifted from one to the other, as we snap on and off our switches to-day. Each holder is also equipped with a little hook by which it may be hung from the back of a chair when one is reading. In grace and simplicity the design closely approaches perfection.

99

HALF-ROUND TABLES were a favorite variation. Sometimes they possessed three legs, sometimes four. The construction often included an apron just under the top. The piece of Zuni pottery and the Navajo rug are not as far from the spirit of early American furniture as we may at first think. [SEE DRAWING 33.]

BECAUSE much of the wood is pine, and because we are interested in the solid turnings and the unusually large proportions of this butterfly table, we are including it here, hastening to note that much has been restored. Both wings and drop leaves are new, as well as the longitudinal stretchers. Their size, however, was known, and the appearance of the table must be not far from what it was originally. The top measures 4 ft., 1 in. round, and is ⅞ in. thick and 2 ft., ½ in. above the floor; the legs are turned from 2⅛ in. square; the stretchers measure 1¾ in. horizontally by 2 in. vertically; and the top rail measures a scant 1¼ in. by 5¾ in. The outside measurements of the frame at the top are 1 ft., 2 in. by 2 ft., 9 in., and at the botton, 1 ft., 7¾ in. by 2 ft., 9 in. The piece is owned by Mr. Oliver E. Williams and is in his Rockport house.

101

IT MUST NOT be supposed that butterfly tables were suddenly and without warning invented. Most of the elements were in current use, but never before had they been put together in exactly that way. Joined stools had splayed frames; gate-leg tables had drop leaves with long and narrow drawers between and oval tops with pivoted supports. It was the agreeable combining of these structural elements that was the stroke of genius.

The wood of this table is maple except for the supporting wings, which are pine, a fact which allows us to include it in the discussion. In the drawing plate we have made a restoration of the feet to give it more nearly its intended proportions. The table here illustrated and drawn to scale is owned by Mr. Henry Ford and may be seen at Longfellow's Wayside Inn at Sudbury. [SEE DRAWING 34.]

8. DESKS

AN INTERESTING SUBJECT that has received but slight comment is the close relation between various articles of furniture at a given period. This, of course, is really no more than is natural, for in furniture of this time it is the structure that gives character; and the building principles used in a chest, for instance, were really the same as those applied to the problem of the desk and scrutoir.

The need of the early settlers for some place to keep their most valuable and personal belongings, recognized in the little compartment or till that appears at one side of nearly every chest, was early met by the desk box. It was a small affair of pine or oak, or sometimes walnut, easily portable, and it served for the storage of books and papers or of the family Bible.

The top was hinged at the back and frequently slanted, either for convenience in writing or to hold the Bible during family prayers, and the more elaborate boxes were carved. Among the carving we recognize the designs that appear on the chests, there being desk box examples even of the localized "Hadley" pattern.

After the middle of the Seventeenth Century, both the flat and the slant top desk box are sometimes found placed upon a frame. In this form they became a chest on frame and a desk on frame respectively. At first they rested upon the frame but were not made a structural part of it. Later they were definitely attached.

The hinges on these pieces, when the top was flat, were almost invariably of the bent wire type, but on the slanting ones, the butterflies were usual. Hinged at the back at first, like the chests from which they developed, there are also found desks, of early date, in which the lid swings from hinges in front and lets down to be supported for the writing surface. For long both ideas were used, but the greater possibilities of the latter assured its final victory. With the lid swinging forward, the writer was kept away from the frame, and the space otherwise occupied by his legs could be filled with drawers. This change occurred toward the end of the Seventeenth Century, when we find ball-foot scrutoirs that really were only chests of drawers with scrutoir tops. The scrutoir, we should mention, was an expensive form of writing desk that appears in the inventories from 1669 on. Its first forms are mere conjectures.

But even this amount of filing space did not satisfy the more important people, for with the new century desks began to be made with cabinet tops, open at first and divided into an array of pigeonholes of various sizes. Later, it was the custom to fit them with wooden doors; and, when the pigeonholes turned into mere book shelves, the doors were made of glass.

The development of these features through the block serpentine desks, into the Sheraton, and finally the Empire styles is an interesting story, but by then the whole spirit had changed and the word "early" may no longer be applied.

102

AS DESK BOXES were primarily intended to keep things in—papers, trinkets, and so on—their tops were at first flat. They were, almost without exception, made just as well as the workmen knew how, and often were decorated in one way or another. The box illustrated here is made entirely of pine. It is dovetailed on the vertical edges and moulded around the bottom with a quarter-round and on the lid with a thumbnail moulding. The hinges are of the staple type. All these features are standard. Variation comes largely in the decoration and in the fact that carved boxes were usually made of oak, a wood of greater dignity and better suited to such treatment. Even this pine box, however, has a show of decoration, for a slight notching may be seen on the four upright edges. When there is no lock, according to Mr. Nutting's reasonable theory, we may suppose that the box contained not valuable documents but a Bible—which was its own protection.

The casement window with its original leaded glass is pine. It came from the same house in Still River, near Harvard, Massachusetts, as did the diamond shaped fixed sash that may be seen in the Ipswich Room of the Boston Museum of Fine Arts. Even the thin wooden sticks that brace the delicate fabric of the glass at the third points are still in place. [SEE DRAWING 35.]

103

QUITE in the spirit of the Seventeenth Century are the construction and the decoration of this desk box. In the first place, it is joined at the vertical edges with a shouldered corner, and the lid, which is a restoration, swings, as did the original, on staple hinges. In the second place, the mouldings run along the grain much like the shadow mouldings of Seventeenth Century wall sheathing, and there is the decorative strip of arches, popular early because it was so easily put on. Each arch is formed by two half circles scratched with a compass, the space between stamped with a curving row of dotted circles, to make which there was used a specially prepared punch. This same punch appears again on what is left of the bevelled projection of the bottom. Another punch, probably just the head of a hand-made nail, decorates the center strip between the two horizontal mouldings. In the house from which this box came there was a spinning wheel decorated with the same scratched and stamped arches—further evidence of its antiquity. All is original except the lid, and all is pine. The little braces across the ends of the lid were invariably of some harder wood, better able to hold out against the tendency of the wide top to warp.

104

THESE TWO DESK BOXES show the use of pine with oak.

In the first one pine is used for both the top and bottom. The box measures 9 in. by 2 ft., 2½ in. by 1 ft., 3 in. It is dated 1675-1700.

The second box is likewise oak in the carved parts, but the top is probably ash, and the bottom pine. The carved decoration still shows black paint, while there are traces of the red paint that formerly covered the uncarved surface. The measurements are 9½ in. by 2 ft., 5 in. by 1 ft., 3½ in., and the date 1650-1700.

Both are in the Metropolitan Museum.

WHEN one finds an authentic box with as early a date as 1683 on it, one is fortunate indeed. Mr. William B. Goodwin, of Hartford, has two such pieces, for he also owns a six-board chest exhibiting a date ten years earlier still. Is not that (1673) the earliest dated American piece known?

THERE are many interesting things to be seen in this photograph besides the carved desk box for which it was taken. In the first place, the great chest, initialled "S. W.," is decorated with very nearly the same shadow moulding as that which appears on the walls of the room. This type of moulding was designed primarily to conceal the joint between two boards placed edge to edge, but its value as pure decoration was also recognized. You often find it run across a wide board, as here, just for the interesting shadows that its blade leaves behind it. Hence the name, "shadow moulding."

Above the box is a very accurate reproduction of the fixed sash with diamond leaded lights that, from all evidence, must have occupied this position in the house in the Seventeenth Century. Irregular, yellow-green glass, with many waves and bubbles in it, was held together by the lead strips which in turn were secured at intervals to oak bars set into the frame of the window if it was a fixed type, as here, and into the sash if it was a casement.

Above the window is a yoke used upon human shoulders in taking sap-buckets to and from the maple trees. Unless one has struggled up to camp with two buckets slopping water into his boot tops at every stride, the advantages of this contrivance can never be appreciated. The writer has seen the same thing accomplished abroad by the use of a light wooden hoop about three feet in diameter. The carrier steps inside the hoop and picks up the buckets with his hands on the outside of the circle.

The desk box came from Bedford, Massachusetts. It is in perfect condition, with no restoration of any kind. It measures 1 ft., 1½ in. wide by 1 ft., 8¼ in. long, by 8 in. high below the lid. Owned by the writer, but its setting is the Browne House at Watertown.

107

THE INSIDE of a desk box was usually perfectly plain, but sometimes we find it divided by partitions into little pigeonholes,
which soon were scalloped decoratively. Then for the first time
it begins to suggest what we think of to-day as being a desk.
Slanting the top is another quite natural step forward. The
smooth flat top must have been a very convenient place on which
to write, but it was eventually thought that a slanting top was
even better. Mrs. Richard T. Fisher, of Weston, Massachusetts,
owns this box.

108

WHEN THE LID is slanted we have for the first time a recognition, in the design, of the box's connection with writing. The sloping top often seemed to call for a thin strip of moulding that should keep papers from sliding to the floor; the back and horizontal part of the top might be provided with a railing. This railing was later developed into shelves, and finally into elaborate glazed cabinets. Dimensions below the lid: 1 ft., 8¾ in. by 1 ft., 4¾ in. by 4½ in. high in front and 7 in. high at the back.

109

ALL DESK BOXES thus far illustrated were designed to rest upon a chest or to be set upon a table, but there were examples, too, built upon frames, and counting thus as furniture of considerable importance. There is a fine example in the Museum at Hartford which we might just as well have included here as with the chests. (Plate 43.)

The idea of the slant-top desk box was sometimes carried out in a modest fashion, much like the six-board chest. The example we show here measures 2 ft. 4½ in. long, 1 ft., 3 in. wide, and 3 ft., 6 in. high. The especially interesting feature we shall discover only when we raise the lid on its butterfly hinges. The inside is not at once a deep well extending down into the first drawer, but a shallow affair formed by a horizontal partition hardly lower than the front of the lid. To reach the well you must go down through a trap door in the horizontal partition. This is one of the tell-tale features of the late Seventeenth Century writing desk. The property of Mr. Albert H. Atkins of West Gloucester.

110

ANOTHER DESK of the "six-board" family. The lid opens on
staple hinges. The early Eighteenth Century mirror, the stool
with splayed legs, and last but not least, the walls of the room,
are to be noticed. The walls are 7 in. logs and date back to the
pioneer days of Rockport, Massachusetts, when Indians had to
be reckoned with. The house is that of Mr. Oliver E. Williams.

III

THIS PINE DESK ON FRAME dates from the first years of the Eighteenth Century. It is a quaint-looking relic, for at one time in its life it was painted a bright blue, which is still very much in evidence everywhere but on the top, where the weather has removed it entirely. When we lift the lid backward on its handsome butterfly hinges, we see inside a very definite though crude attempt at style. There are five arched pigeonholes at the back, with a row of three drawers underneath. In the Museum of the Rhode Island School of Design.

112

THE INGENIOUS CABINETMAKER who first hinged the lid at the front did away with the last serious difficulty. The desk shown here, in general appearance, is not so very unlike the one in Providence just discussed. But by swinging the lid toward him, the craftsman effected three things. In the first place, he made the desk comfortable. There is now plenty of room for one's knees. In the second place, he brought in the possibility of filling in the space beneath the desk with drawers, clear down to the ground—and this was soon to be done. In the third place, he freed the closed lid from considerations of writing. It might now take what slope it wanted and be worked more easily into the design of the whole—and this, too, was soon accomplished. This desk of pine, with a maple frame, measures 2 ft. in width and 3 ft., 2½ in. in height. The writing surface is 2 ft., 2½ in. above the floor. It is in the American Wing of the Metropolitan Museum.

113

THE MOULDING PLANE in such favour in the early years of the Eighteenth Century places this desk with a fair degree of accuracy. The lid, when open, rests on very nearly square arms; for it was some time before the efficiency of a deep and narrow arm was recognized. Similarly, early floor joists were roughly square in section, whereas to-day we use 2 in. by 10 in. Beneath the writing surface and above the main drawer is a well, reached, as is characteristic of the period, through an opening above. Its door slides under the two center drawers.

It is a pine desk, 3 ft., 7 in. high over all. The frame is maple, measuring 1 ft., 6 in. by 2 ft., 3 in. by 2 ft., 1 in. high. The legs are turned·from 1¾ in. square and the stretchers made from ¾ in. by 1¾ in. The brasses are modern but correct in pattern. The piece is owned by Mr. Henry Ford, and it is in the Wayside Inn in Sudbury, Massachusetts.

THIS BEAUTIFUL DESK is made entirely of pine, even the finely turned legs. The arms that pull out to hold the writing surface are high and narrow, giving a date toward the end of the period of the drop handle, of which we see two used on the drawer front. Mrs. De Witt C. Howe is the owner.

ON A RIBBON at the bottom of the seal of the Commonwealth of Massachusetts is the motto, "*Ense petit placidam sub libertate quietem,*" which becomes, in a schoolboy's graceful, musical translation: "By means of a sword he seeks peaceful quiet under liberty." The last two Latin words of this sentiment appear on the under side of this schoolmaster's desk. Just what the motto's official interpretation was we do not venture to state; but somehow it suggests the old-time relationship between boys and master rather than the new! The beauty and the cleverness of the desk are quite apparent in the photograph. It measures at the base, 2 ft., 9¼ in. wide by 1 ft., 10 in. deep by 2 ft., 2½ in. from the floor to the writing surface. The property of Mr. Henry Davis Sleeper, of Gloucester.

116

JUST at a time when the writer was wondering if there were not to be found desks with high open shelves above, he saw this very perfect example, all in pine, and with a very aristocratic pedigree going back to the noted cabinetmakers of Manchester, Massachusetts. It is a fact that there are few untouched steps in the various developments that we are tracing. Some steps were very lightly trod upon, but the climb was seldom attempted two steps at a time, and there probably never was any single step entirely skipped. The advantages of having doors to close over these shelves assured their introduction, yet even the finest panelling or glazing could be no more interesting than this frank, orderly partitioning of space. The boldness of it reminds one of an architect's library, especially designed to hold the high sets, no one of which is the same size as any other. We are indebted to Miss Teresa V. Carey, of Boston, for permission to take this photograph.

117

HERE, in this pine desk with cabinet top, we see the solid doors predicted in the previous photograph. Every part of the piece is heavily constructed; the wide door at the bottom, the upright boards of the cabinet top, the chunky cornice. The consistency of it more than makes up in interest for what it lacks in delicacy. The property of Mrs. Amos Little, of Marlboro, Massachusetts.

118

SHAKER PIECES are apt to be of exceedingly straightforward construction. This little desk, for instance, though beautifully dovetailed and cut out at the base, has not a moulding on it. It is in the office of Strickland, Blodget, and Law, in Boston. [SEE DRAWING 36.]

HERE is an interesting example of a type that is often spoken of as a school-master's desk, but which really would be too uncomfortable to sit at for the long hours that go with that profession. Storekeeper's desk would be a better term, for one could write down occasional items while standing at it. This example is owned by Mr. E. Gordon Parker of Cambridge, Massachusetts.

I 2 0

IN THIS sort of desk, not often seen, the slant of the lid has disappeared entirely. When closed, the piece appears as a chest of
drawers. The front of the top division, however, drops forward
on curious quarter-circle brass supports, and suddenly you have
a desk at your disposal! It is built entirely of pine in this instance,
and painted in imitation of some rarer wood. The brasses and
the serpentine top place it in Revolutionary times. Mr. Allen
French, of Concord, is the owner.

9. SHELVES AND CUPBOARDS

ALL THE ACCIDENTAL LEDGES that the frame of the Seventeenth Century house provided held, without doubt, their full quota of ornaments and household wares. But there were not enough of them. We can see evidences of the shelving that was early built to hold and to display the array of glass, china, earthenware, wooden, pewter, and even silver utensils that were in daily use. Soon, owing to the pride with which each family looked upon its equipment, more attention was paid to these shelves. They were made into definite and movable pieces of furniture, the sides scalloped into rhythmic successions of arcs or scrolls. Racks, hanging from the walls, shone with much used pewter spoons. Small sets of shelves hung like the racks; larger sets, known as dressers, stood against the walls between windows or at corners where they would be most convenient.

At first these dressers were nothing but open shelves beautifully patterned, with often a slight setback at table height for convenience. But the usefulness of drawers and enclosed cupboards was soon recognized, and their inevitable introduction came about, first in the lower portion. In this form the piece is now in much demand.

The tendency to enclose the shelves did not stop there, however, and before long doors became the rule for the upper portion as well. This, of course, eliminated the scalloped side boards. Beauty was elbowed out by utility. A dresser of this less picturesque type is nowadays usually converted into one of an earlier type before it goes upon the market of genuine antiques!

Dressers belonged to the kitchen. The kitchen, or "hall," as it was called, was originally the main room of the house. It was there the family ate its meals and gathered in the evening. But as the two functions of cooking and dining became separated, there were built cupboards designed solely for the display of the very finest plate and ware. This type of cupboard was destined to find its way into a position of formal importance in the panelling of the Colonial dining room.

At first, it was merely a side wall cupboard, a narrow dresser consisting of doors below and shelves above the table height. When, instead of scalloping the side pieces, faceboards were added, the inclusion of the cupboard within the panelling of the room was but a matter of time. The cupboard was found to fit economically into corners and it was soon made the full height of the room and took the room's cornice for its own.

As, toward the middle of the Seventeenth Century, architecture lost its informalities and took on the carefully planned symmetry of Revolutionary times, the cupboard was adapted to the new fashions by being sunk flush into the wall, usually filling up the space that is created beside a fireplace by the thickness of the chimney. Here, either one of a pair or balanced by some other architectural feature, it was provided with panelled doors or doors of glass, and became an important part of a dignified architectural composition.

121

A SPOON RACK with a box for knives below. Knives not being of pewter, and forks at first not even being known, it was the spoons that were made much of by being put on individual display. This rack belongs to Mr. Henry Ford and is in Longfellow's Wayside Inn at Sudbury. [SEE DRAWING 37.]

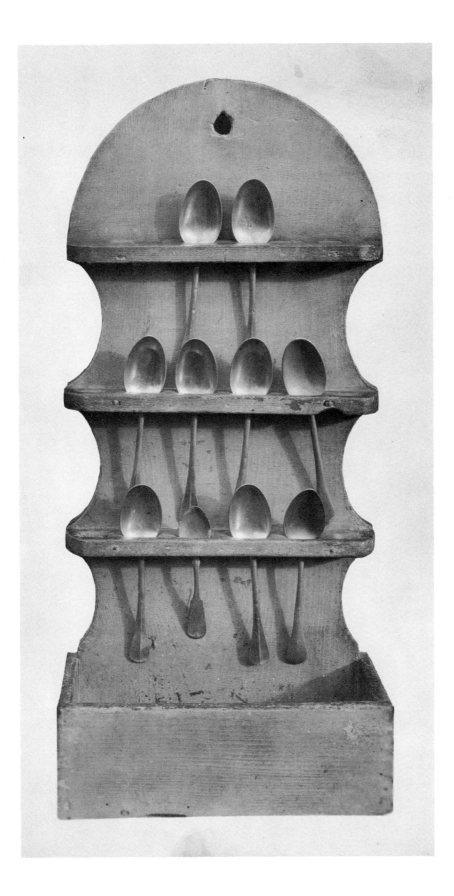

122

WHEN a little piece is carved in this geometric fashion we at once think of Pennsylvania. Some day we shall perhaps be able to trace the story back across the water. Yet from the very simplicity of it, might we not expect it occasionally to have been the spontaneous expression of an individual? This beautiful rack also belongs to Mr. Henry Ford.

THE CARVER, R.S., was also meticulous enough to give us the date when he made this spoon rack—1783. He got this lacework effect by the use of just two tricks of the chisel.

Mr. John M. Woolsey is the owner.

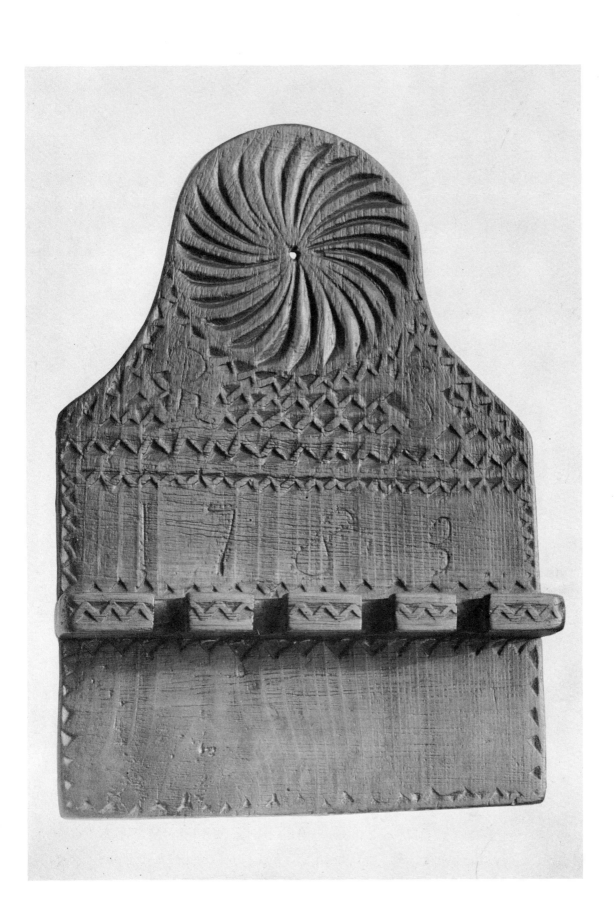

I 24

THE MAKER of this rack showed all his tricks. Mr. John M. Woolsey, the owner, says that both this piece and the preceding one
are from New England.

125

A KNIFE BOX. In form, it seems admirably suited to hold a handful of knives with blades taking up little space in comparison with that required by the handles. The scalloping of the sides raises the box at once from a piece of no interest to one of considerable appeal. There is still in evidence a coat of red-orange paint, even now far brighter than the permanent red stain more usually found.

126

THE IMMEDIATE DEMAND for shelving must have been met by the construction of just such shelves as these. They are new, but the depth and the length and the spacing were all planned from unmistakable marks in the framework of the room just across the entry, so we are assured of a very accurate picture of Seventeenth Century conditions. The wood is ⅞ in. pine throughout. The boards are about 7¼ in. in width, which is the width of the corner post and the second floor sill against which they stop. Practically all of the pieces of ware are wooden—plates, spoons, pitchers, buckets, and porringers.

On the right, hanging from a nail, is an adjustable rushlight from which in turn hangs a betty lamp. Either light might have been sufficient to prolong a discussion until well into the night, but five hundred of them would have been required in taking this photograph. In the house of Mr. Albert H. Atkins, at West Gloucester.

127

THESE old leather-covered books and the pine frame-work of the shelves have the mutual sympathy of old friends. This photograph was taken at the "Village Green Shop" in Ipswich, an old house belonging to Mrs. Parker Whittemore.

128

A SET OF HANGING SHELVES like this is useful for displaying a variety of things, the sole requirements, perhaps, being that they shall be reasonably small and that they be handsome! This particular set was built to fit into a corner, so only the outer side board was scalloped. [SEE DRAWING 28.]

129

THERE is nothing cramped about the design of these corner shelves. The curves in every case are generous sweeps, perfectly adapted to the easily worked pine. For oak the design would be quite different. It is worth noticing how fine a curve could be drawn down through the projecting points of the side boards. Without a doubt that line was the first one to be drawn upon the wood. The narrowing shelves and the diminishing brackets were laid out from that line as a basis. The wood is ⅝ in. throughout; the over all measurements are 2 ft., 4 in. high, and 12¾ in. wide on the sides. There is a slight bevel on the under side of each shelf that prevents it from appearing too heavy. It is hard to make a rule by which we can understand the difference between pleasing and scatter-brained designs of this sort. Perhaps a maker has a better chance of success if he takes one or two perfectly understandable motifs and uses them in a rhythmic way, as here, than if he gets excited over the fact that he has all the curves in Christendom at his disposal.

The two lower shelves have old glassware upon them. The glasses on the two upper shelves are relatively modern. The photographer made use of a clever trick to bring out the cutting on the sides of the little glass bottle. First, he rubbed Bon Ami on the surface and let it dry. With a rag he then polished it off, leaving the white in the star design, with very evident results.

130

THIS SET OF WALL SHELVES probably had three more drawers at
the top just like the ones below. Mr. A. G. Baldini, of Wakefield,
is the owner. [SEE DRAWING 39.]

I 3 I

IF ONLY we could prove the New England origin of this particular piece it would settle a much disputed point. Are the water benches that we find here indigenous, or have they worked their way north for higher prices in a locality where they are "very rare?" Pennsylvania is their natural territory. The water bench provided shelves for the buckets of water that were in continuous demand about the kitchen before piping came into use. This attractive little example is owned by Mr. Jerome Preston, of West Hingham, Massachusetts. [SEE DRAWING 40.]

MOST WATER BENCHES, because of the coarseness of their scale, need large pieces upon them to be shown to advantage. The scale of the curved sides is certainly emphasized here by the huge pewter platters. Mr. A. G. Baldini, of Wakefield, is the owner. [SEE DRAWING 41.]

THIS PRESS CUPBOARD is one of the most beautiful pieces of pine that one is privileged to see. It is a translation into more modest wood of one of the more elaborate oak cupboards that were the possession of the wealthy Colonists of the Puritan period. It is far from a copy. Possibly consciously, more probably just naturally, the design is everywhere simplified. Excepting the two posts, which are ash, every piece of wood is pine. Some of it an inch in thickness, as is the shelf at the setback, some of it ⅞ in., as the two side boards, but most of it—doors, panels, and all applied mouldings, a full half inch. The plane with which the panel mouldings were run was also used on both with-the-grain edges of the doors, but not across them. One usually finds a reluctance to put the wooden planes to such a test. The cupboard measures 4 ft., 2 in. in height by 1 ft., 7¾ in. wide by 3 ft., 6½ in. long. Upon the card descriptive of the piece, which is on exhibition in the Wallace Nutting Collection of the Morgan Museum in Hartford, there appears the following:

"The name 'poor man's cupboard' has sometimes been applied to these fine specimens. Their existence is a very human and amusing illustration of the fact that all classes of people wish to follow the style, and some who could not afford the stately oak cupboard thought it worth while to own a humble pine imitation built of boards without a joined frame."

134

HERE we have the dresser half way advanced from the open shelves (Plate 126) to its final stage of being enclosed both top and bottom. "H"-hinges, or butterfly, or less frequently, staple, are used on dresser doors. Wooden knobs—or nothing at all— and sometimes a wooden catch turning on a nail completed the primitive "hardware." Mr. I. Sack, of Boston, is the owner.

ON THIS DRESSER there is no evidence of there ever having been any more efficient means of opening either the doors of the drawers beyond a dexterous use of the finger nails. We suspect that the hinges are a restoration, for they are larger than one would expect to find. This piece, with its beautiful collection of Pennsylvania slipware, was photographed in the King Hooper house at Marblehead and is owned by Mr. H. F. Du Pont, of Delaware. [SEE DRAWINGS 42 AND 43.]

136

THE DRESSER is, of course, entirely of pine, and its smooth, reddish surfaces make the softest background imaginable for the pewter and wooden utensils. The height is 7 ft., the length 5 ft., 11 in., and the depth over all 1 ft., 2½ in.

On the top shelf at the back there is just discernible a wooden bowl, three inches deep. In the course of time the wood has shrunk so much across the grain that it now has two diameters —1 ft., 9 in., if you measure with the run of the wood, and 1 ft., 8⅛ in. across the grain.

On the right of the dresser, in the corner, is to be seen a supply of candles hanging from the wooden spikes that project from a rectangular pine board 1 in. thick, 10 in. wide, and 1 ft., 3½ in. tall. The spikes are 6 in. long, and ⅜ in. in diameter, and taper to a point. They are staggered in their positions so that the upper rows of candles may hang without touching the rows below.

The long "X"-trestle table in the foreground used to be the official dining piece of the Hopkinton Poor Farm. We doubt if it was ever before surrounded by such a beautiful group of chairs. The photograph is taken in Mrs. De Witt C. Howe's country house in Hopkinton, New Hampshire.

137

IN THE old kitchen of the Wayside Inn at Sudbury Mr. Henry Ford has placed this perfectly preserved dresser and its panoply of shining pewter. The scroll-cut sides are quite different from the more usual treatment of alternating convex and concave arcs.

NOTHING can show off pewter more effectively than pine. This wall cupboard is a free-standing piece, yet in the narrow front pieces of the upper section we see suggested the possibilities of sinking the cupboard into the wall and treating the two as one surface. The cornice is unusually heavy, and the feet simple, but very effective. The photograph was taken in Longfellow's Wayside Inn, Sudbury.

139

WHEN the old kitchen of the Barker House at Pembroke was rescued and moved to Mr. Sleeper's house at East Gloucester, this slant-front wall cupboard came with it. The sides, 1 ft., 4½ in. wide, extend straight to a height of 2 ft., 6 in. and then taper to the top, which is 1 ft. wide, 5 ft., 10½ in. above the floor, and 2 ft., 1 in. long, exclusive of the very heavy cornice that projects 4 in. in a height of 4¼ in.

The ratchet candle stand came from Waterbury, Connecticut, and the lantern, whose head is bevelled and hollowed out, came from Rowley, Massachusetts.

140

WHEN the closing-in process spread to the upper as well as the lower sections of the dresser such pieces as this resulted. They afforded, of course, far better protection to the ware with which they were filled, and might still be very handsome. This dresser shows itself to be later than those illustrated previously, by the cast iron hinges, (which were not made before the Revolution) and by the detailing of the panels, in which the bevel springs directly from the rails and stiles without the quarter-round moulding. The owner is Mrs. Parker Whittemore, of Ipswich, Massachusetts.

141

ORIGINALLY this wall cupboard was three full panels high. Rats and mice and heavy boots must have worn away the bottom until the day finally came when it was sawed off level to get a fresh start. In its present proportions, in spite of the very beautiful texture of the unpainted pine, it is indisputably squat and heavy. Yet it has unusual interest. Examine the panelling of the doors and you will see why. The work has been done in mediæval fashion—by someone who in those days, perhaps, was "a gentleman of the old school,"—for the moulding on the horizontal rails of the doors runs all the way across, while on the vertical pieces, or stiles, to save complications at the corners, it was cut only across the middle, fading out to nothing at either end. This is the way oak panelling was put together in Elizabethan times, but the method was very seldom used in America, except in some of the earliest oak chests. Mrs. Winfield Shaw of New Boston, New Hampshire, the owner, found the cupboard in a house near-by.

142

THE ESPECIAL GRACE of this wall cupboard is at once apparent. It is more lightly constructed than most, the wood ranging between ⅝ in. and ¾ in. when usually the range is between ¾ in. and a full inch, and this difference is reflected in the design most strikingly where, at the bottom of the front, the feet become but the width of the ¾ in. side pieces. The outside measurements are 6 ft., 5 in. tall, 2 ft., 4 in. long, and 1 ft., 6 in. wide.

On the shelves is a collection of painted wooden animals that came from a farm in Waldoboro, Maine. There are horses, oxen, sheep, and little farm tools, all done in toy scale.

The decorated box on top of the cupboard is American Indian from near Bennington, Vermont.

This photograph was taken in Mr. Henry D. Sleeper's house at East Gloucester.

143

ON THE GROUND FLOOR of Mr. Henry D. Sleeper's East Gloucester house he has included the kitchen frame and panelling
and the old fireplace from the Barker House at Pembroke, Massachusetts, which, until it was torn down, held the honor of
being the oldest house in the country, built in 1628, an honor
now held by the Fairbanks House at Dedham, built in 1636.
The wall cupboard, with its elaborate arched and crossed panelling, shown with this Barker House room as a setting, came
from Danbury, Connecticut. It is relatively low, 5 ft., 10 in, and
has a length of 3 ft., 4 in. and a width of 1 ft., 7 in.

144

ABOVE the walnut chest of drawers hangs a little pine cupboard. The arched glass panels, through which we get a glimpse of still more pewter, give the piece great distinction, even though it is a lone example—that is, not one of a general type. The measurements are 10½ in. by 2 ft., 2 in. at the top, and a height of 2 ft. The glass is cut square across the top and the rebate holding it, of course, follows the glass rather than the shape of the opening at this point. The date is given as 1690-1730 on the card that stands upon it in the Wallace Nutting Collection in the Morgan Museum at Hartford.

145

THIS CUPBOARD came from the neighbourhood of Brattleboro, Vermont. Inside, it is painted a dull red, outside, a light neutral green. It was originally built into the side walls of the room, and the main cornice of the room was continued across its three faces. Unfortunately, the writer could not get these top mouldings when he bought the piece. [SEE DRAWING 44.]

THE SCALE of the lovely design of this cupboard is admirably consistent. One wishes he knew how the cornice was originally moulded—whether or not the same simplicity was maintained. Recently the cupboard has been built into one of the rooms in the American Wing of the Metropolitan Museum.

THIS CORNER CUPBOARD, like most of the dressers, was designed as a movable piece of furniture. It may be pointed out that the same alternating concave and convex arches that are so often used to scallop the sides of the dressers are used here on the front boards, and there is additional scalloping on the shelves themselves. The projection of the corner post into the room usually meant that the back corner of the cupboard had to be cut off in one way or another to allow for it.

The rhyme on the pitcher reads:

> Let the wealthy and great
> Roll in splendor and state
> I envy them not I declare it
> I eat my own lamb—
> My own chickens and ham
> I shear my own fleece and I ware it
> I have lambs I have bowers
> I have fruits I have flowers
> The lark is my morning alarmer
> So jolly boys now—
> Here's God speed the plough
> Long life and success to the farmer.

On the other side we read:

> Mary Hayward
> Farmer
> Sandhurst-Kent

Miss Katrina Kipper, of Accord, is the owner of the cupboard, and of the lustre and china ware. [SEE DRAWING 45.]

148

THIS UNUSUAL CORNER CUPBOARD measures 7 ft. high; the side faces have a width of 6¾ in., and the front face one of 3 ft., 5½ in. The back is circular, giving the cupboard a depth, including the cornice moulding, of 1 ft., 8½ in.; ¾ in. wood is used throughout.

The joint stool and the candlestand are not of pine, but belong in the historical setting, as do the kegs and tankard above.

The corner of the Shaker Room of Mrs. John C. Spring's house at West Gloucester.

149

THE MOST interesting features of this cupboard are the widening of the architrave about the open shelves, and the little slide, hardly noticeable in the photograph, supposedly there to be pulled out to hold a candle when the mistress of the house was arranging the china. The cupboard is 7 ft. high, 3 ft., 9 in. wide, and 2 ft., 11 in. high up to the candle shelf. Right almost at the meeting place of four towns — Lexington, Bedford, Lincoln, and Concord — there stood until quite recently a very fine old house, slowly dropping to pieces. The photograph shows a corner cupboard from that house, saved, along with some other pieces of interior finish, and later given to the United States National Museum by Dr. and Mrs. Arthur M. Greenwood of Marlborough, Massachusetts.

150

ANY LITTLE unused angle gave just the opportunity that was needed for a set of shelves. Just think how near this little triangle must have come to being boarded over for its natural life! Fortunately, the man who planned the house in West Oxford, Massachusetts was an ingenious person, as well as being a skillful designer. Little did he guess that his panelling would be removed into the Boston Museum of Fine Arts, after two hundred years of service in its first location!

151

FILLING up the space in the thickness of the wall caused by the chimney, one often finds a cupboard. In this case the cupboard is very definitely worked into the design of the wall. Here we see the new styles supplanting the faint echoes of mediæval traditions. Stile and rail panelling in place of sheathing; boxed beams and cornice mouldings in place of the rough-hewn and exposed frame that we find in houses of the Seventeenth Century; classical pilasters enriching and emphasizing the focal centre of the room, where the problem would previously have solved itself without self-conscious planning and reference to a *Builder's Companion*. Attention may be called to some other points suggested by the photograph. The muntins, or wooden bars of the glass door, are wide, probably fully an inch and a quarter. Modern muntins and those typical of the Nineteenth Century are much thinner, for we are able to make them more efficiently and thus meet the demand for a less interrupted view. But there is a distinct loss in effect. An old sash, barred with fat muntins and flashing iridescently like a soap bubble with hand-made glass, is very satisfying. In this room there is no mantel shelf. Above the wide fireplaces of the century previous there was often a slight ledge; over the smaller cement or tile-faced openings that soon were characteristic of the Eighteenth Century there was a mantel shelf such as we know to-day. But for a few years in between there was no obvious location for the household ornaments. The emphasis was on the panelling itself, which was often, as here, raised elaborately from its frame, and on the deep bolection moulding that enclosed the fire. The shouldered arch motif, although new to panelling at this time, had been seen in the decoration of chests during the century before. The photograph was taken in the Metropolitan Museum of the room from Newington, Connecticut.

10. FINISH

WHAT WAS THE FINISH on these pieces of furniture, and on the panelling of the walls of the contemporary houses? Much of the early work, without doubt, was kept scrubbed clean, giving the wood the beautiful soft texture that it naturally thus acquires. Into this neutral background the wrought-iron hardware of the corner cupboards or the six-panel doors blended perfectly. In many of the taverns and the finer houses, however, there was used, from very early times, a dull red stain—Indian Red, or Venetian Red pigment mixed with skimmed milk—that sank far into the grain of the wood and became permanent. Probably it represents an attempt to cover over the knots that are inevitably found in pine. We can still see this colour on the walls of the old bar of the Wayside Inn in Sudbury, Massachusetts, and we find it upon many chests and other old pieces on which it has remained for nearly three centuries. We often find it after the laborious process of removing five or six coats of paint. It may be noted that the names of varnishers appear in contemporary records, from 1680, along with those of joiners, turners, upholsterers, and drapers.

In the early inventories there is mention of paint on chairs. "One green chair," "three blue chairs," and so on, we run across, as early as the middle of the Seventeenth Century, along with the red-stained furniture just mentioned, but whether or not this same paint was used on the beams and wall boarding it is hard to prove. Governor Eaton's "green chamber" and "blue chamber," alluded to in 1658, may possibly have referred to the panelling, but more probably to the window hangings and the upholstery, which were a regular part of the furnishing of a house from the middle of the Seventeenth Century.

Although the records leave us in this uncertain state of mind, can we not put considerable trust in the argument that as walls were painted in colors in England during the Middle Ages, there were in all probability some houses finished so here during the prevalence of the mediæval spirit of building?

Men of means came more and more to follow the fashion across the water. The Renaissance, long delayed, was changing the character of English architecture under the able guidance of such men as Sir Christopher Wren (1632-1723), and the architecture of the American Colonies was not long in accepting the new style. The Roman orders had arrived, and their use was a problem that provided designers with both labour and entertainment for about a hundred and fifty years.

It was during the early Seventeen Hundreds, when Anne was Queen of England, that, we learn, many panelled rooms were painted a dull green, with the mouldings picked out in gold. The same sort of gilding was done in Boston in the magnificent Clark-Frankland house, built probably about the middle of the Eighteenth Century, but now destroyed.

Other colors were used, too, as we see in the extremely interesting description of the house of a George Tilley, advertised in the Boston *Gazette* of September 18, 1753. It has eight rooms in it, seven of which are fire rooms; "four of said Rooms is cornish'd, and the house is handsomely painted throughout, one of the Rooms is painted Green, another Blue, one Cedar and one Marble; the other four a Lead color, the Garrets are handsomely plaistered." The record is not surprising to anyone who has stripped layer after layer of color from an old panelled room.

But what about white paint? We know that it was the custom among the Dutch settlers of New Amsterdam to whitewash the walls and ceilings of their houses, and that this same fashion existed also in New England. A house advertised in the Boston *Gazette* of November 8-15, 1736, boasted "the upper chambers well Plaistered and white wash'd." The "white chamber," mentioned in Governor William Phipps' house as early as 1696, was more probably whitewashed than painted. It is the writer's personal belief that white was but one of a number of colors used popularly until fairly well past the middle of the Eighteenth Century. With the development of Colonial society and the spread of prosperity, social life made greater and greater call for brighter fashions. It was then that one walked through blue-green, yellow, orange, and white rooms, each room furnished in a subtle composition of colors making a worthy background for the elegant social life of the time.

Of these brilliant hues, white was, of course, the one that lent itself most naturally to the splendour of midnight and early morning festivities, and in the end it seems to have been accepted as the proper treatment for a panelled room, especially one of formal character. Rooms of lesser importance, and indeed many of the most pretentious as well, were wall-papered after about 1750, and white proved itself again to be an agreeable choice for painting such wood finish as there might be.

Before leaving the subject of painting we should mention the imitation graining that was done so beautifully in the Eighteenth Century, and is done so dreadfully today. The Abbot House in Andover, Massachusetts shows the art at its very best. It was common in England and Scotland from very early times, and was copied here spasmodically, never reaching the point of being a rigid fashion. A crude form, possibly an imitation of snakewood, more likely merely an attempt to break up a plain surface, is the streak-daubing in black over a coat of red paint. It was not done on walls, but was not uncommon on minor pieces of furniture such as chests and footstools.

Walls were painted in some of the country districts, in imitation of the expensive landscape papers of the more prosperous towns. Such painting was seldom done on wood, but was a water color or tempera painting done directly on the plastered wall. The subjects were apt to be local scenes, fields, buildings, and animal life, drawn, as it were, directly from the originals to be seen beyond the windowpane. Such decoration is traceable up into the first half of the Nineteenth Century.

At first, flooring, like the walls, had only the unpremeditated finish given it by constant scouring. Over this was swept a thin sprinkling of sand which, in the less used rooms, might have a fanciful pattern brushed into it. Later floors were often painted in reds and browns and yellows, or spattered in colours over an undercoating. A black painted baseboard sometimes gave a practical border to the room. Such floors, still often sanded, were the custom until 1750, when carpets became general.

In spite of a few boldly patterned exceptions, such as that in the Buckman Tavern in Lexington, ceilings seldom received much more than a secondary attention. What wood there might be exposed was treated to match the walls, while the plaster was left in its natural color. The "stucco paper for ceilings" advertised in 1760 can have met with but little favor. Nor does the more familiar paper with the little silver stars on a white ground seem to have gained more than passing appreciation.

II. SIGNS AND WEATHER VANES

SIGNS AND WEATHER VANES are alike in being so decorative, and in depending so much for their effect upon bright colors and upon interesting outline against the sky.

The practice of attracting the public's attention to one's business is almost as old as man. We find signs used, not merely since the Middle Ages, but in the great days of Rome, of Greece, and even of Egypt. The idea, therefore, was not a new one when tavern keepers of this country in the Seventeenth Century hung up great painted planks to steer both travellers and townsmen in their direction. Nor was the shoe-maker or the butcher originating a custom when he followed suit, and as the Eighteenth Century got under way houses of persons of every calling were marked by signboards competing with one another for public attention.

Popular opinion eventually turned upon the scheme, for apparently the signs were beginning to injure the landscapes of not only this country, but of England and of the Continent as well, just as we are reaching a similar conclusion to-day about the roadside advertising of cigarettes and tires. We find, in England first, as early as 1669, attempts to limit the size of a sign and its projection on the street; then nearly a hundred years later in both Paris and London laws compelling signs to be fixed flat against the wall or removed; and in 1770 Philadelphia restricted the use of signboards to tavern keepers alone. In other parts of the country, however, the custom has persisted without interruption. The Antiquarian Society in Concord, Massachusetts, can show you a wooden razor, about five feet long when open, that proclaimed the trade of John Wesson from about the year 1850 on, and residents of Boston have long admired the gilded teakettle that spurts steam from its colossal spout above the heads of passers-by in Scollay Square. Incidentally, it was at about the time of the decline in favor of the signboards that there was begun the numbering of houses on a street, and by 1805, London, for example, had made house numbering compulsory.

In the decoration of a man's sign he saw a great chance to make a popular appeal in the colors used and in the subjects and mottoes chosen. The innkeeper often settled upon a well-groomed horse, or a coach-and-four, or (frequently) a punchbowl, adding his own name and the tavern's date, which, as with old wine, was a point to be considered. If the inn or its owner was fortunate enough to have a name that could be depicted, it would be the artist's inspiration. Who could doubt what the sign of the Black Horse Tavern must have looked like, or that of the Washington Hotel?

A letter published in the *Spectator* of April 2, 1710, remarks by way of advice:

"When the name gives an occasion for an ingenious sign post, I would likewise advise the owner to take that opportunity of letting the world know who he is. It would have been ridiculous for the ingenious Mrs. Salmon to have lived at the sign of the trout; for which reason she has erected before her house the figure of the fish that is her namesake. Mr. Bell has likewise distinguished himself by a device of the same nature...."

We find the influence attached to a worthy character often sought, even when the connection is faint or nil. Portraits of Washington, Franklin, Hancock, Lafayette, William Pitt, and General Wolfe are frequently seen. The British lion, too, was popular, although in one instance, at least, after the Revolutionary War, the Golden Lion had to end his days under the incognito of the Yellow Cat!

Figures of heraldry, ideas from the Bible, specially composed verses, local and exotic animals, all worked their way onto the signboards and were twisted and combined with sometimes most amazing and impossible results. The sign of the Goat and Compass had evolved through generations of the careless muttering of the motto "God encompasseth us"; the sign showing an uncivilized man standing beside a bell was originally "La Belle Sauvage."

Further explanation of the unintelligible mixture is given by the writer to the *Spectator:* that

> "It is usual for a young tradesman, at his first setting up, to add to his sign that of the master whom he served; as the husband, after marriage, gives a place to his mistress's arms in his own coat. This I take to have given rise to many of those absurdities which are committed over our heads;..."

This custom he would regulate, and also he

> "would enjoin every shop to make use of a sign which bears some affinity to the wares in which it deals .... A cook should not live at the boot, nor a shoemaker at the roasted pig...."

He suggests that as a remedy there should be appointed a "Superintendent of all such figures and devices."

> "For want of such an officer, there is nothing like sound literature and good sense to be met with in those objects, that are everywhere thrusting themselves out to the eye, and endeavouring to become visible. Our streets are filled with blue boars, black swans, and red lions; not to mention flying pigs and hogs in armour, with many other creatures more extraordinary than any in the deserts of Africa."

Some of these queer associations have established themselves thoroughly in our modern life. Who does not know that three balls are the sign of a pawnbroker; or that a striped pole indicates a barber shop? But few know why. The gilded mortar and pestle still signify a drug store, although we are rapidly having to change our ideas of what is there for sale.

The amount of skill displayed in the painting of these early signs varied greatly. Usually the free hand work was crude. Horses' legs proved beyond the powers of most artists, while the lettering attained a very high degree of excellence. But there are instances in the Colonies where real artists, like Benjamin West, the Peales, and Gilbert Stuart, were reputed to have done the work. Whether such is true or not, the painting must have been exceedingly well done or the report would never have attained favor.

So much for the painted decoration. A great deal of character, however, came from the proportions and outlines of the signs.

In the first place, these signboards were almost without exception of vertical design. This was logical enough, for such a shape provided a maximum of display surface with a minimum length required on the supporting arm or bracket. Besides being thoroughly logical, this shape is a pleasing one from an æsthetic point of view. Picture frames, windows, books, doorways are just a few of the many things that are apt to be made approximately a square and a half in height.

If the sign was a simple rectangle it would be framed, like a picture, with applied mouldings, on both front and back if the painting appeared on both faces.

Most signboards, however, were more elaborate than that. Usually above and below the rectangular applied moulding the main panel was extended and scalloped much as it was in some of the mirrors, but in simpler outline, owing to the greater thickness of the plank. The curving of the upper part took some form suggested by a pediment, or a broken arch, or a pair of scrolls. But as there was little or no precedent to follow for the bottom curving, the designers had to fall back upon their ingenuity, with results that were not always so satisfactory.

The grander signs were flanked by columns or turned posts, framed into the design purely for the decorative effect. The cross pieces, by means of which these were held in place, were, when the sign hung from the column's heads, tenoned into them. When the sign hung from the corners of the main board, the columns were dowelled into the cross pieces. There are some exceptions to this rule, but they are not as sound structurally.

It is interesting to note how much this type of signboard resembles the bracket clock usually associated with the name of Eli Terry. This master clockmaker, born in 1772, may quite possibly have been influenced by signs that had hung for generations before the inns and shops about him.

Why, one might ask, are there no signboards flanked by half columns set flat against the main slab, similar to so many mirrors and clocks of the Empire period? The reason, without doubt, is that the builder saw too clearly the possibilities of getting his design silhouetted against the sky—why should he waste the profile of his turning by backing it with wood?

Rarely one runs across a carved sign. It is rather remarkable that there were so few of them, when one considers how great an amount of lasting beauty was to be had by a few extra hours of work. Often the design seems to have been carved in very low relief, when in reality what has happened is that the unpainted background has been worn away by the weather, leaving lettering and painted figures on a veritable plateau. The commercial slogan of "save the surface and you save all," is true indeed.

The construction always started with a wide pine board, usually about an inch and a quarter thick. On and about this were assembled the mouldings and turnings required to make up the design. Hanging was accomplished by means of wrought-iron bars, flattened at one end to give a good bearing on the wood, beaten into an eye at the other to provide means of attachment to the bracket or horizontal limb.

Some signs, of course, were fixed flat against the walls of buildings, but most of them carried their advertising on both sides and hung out at right angles over the passers-by. The supporting arm might be a stout wooden stick projecting from the wall or from a post; or it might be a wrought-iron bracket, properly braced, projecting in similar fashion; or it might be the limb of a tree. Occasionally two posts set in the ground, with a third member put across from one top to the other constituted the necessary framework. The board always swung ponderously on its supports and must have done much complaining on windy nights.

The word "vane" was formerly spelled "fane," which means pennon or flag. This would indicate pretty clearly what were the earliest ancestors of all the arrows, ships, roosters, horses, and so on that have pointed into the wind for the last several centuries.

From almost the first, the weather vane was accepted as a chance to invade the fields of the imagination. Dragons flew aloft; barnyard animals left their proper plane and soared above the gables and the ridges of outbuildings; fishes swam among the clouds. Beneath them sometimes were the four points of the compass, but while these metal indicators were the usual company of the more elaborate wrought-iron vanes, both in this country and in England, they were by no means a necessary adjunct to the wooden creatures we are considering. The unsophisticated farmer knew what weather to expect from a certain quarter without needing to give it the name of east or west.

On nearly all the weather creatures that we find to-day the evidence of realistic painting, though faint, is unmistakable. They were invariably made to stand out, with their best foot forward and in their gayest hues.

It was not often possible to make the weight balance and still have an unbalanced surface offering its resistance to the wind—as was, of course, necessary for the proper operation of it. But in spite of this constant wearing against the rod, the holes seldom show any greater wear than do other parts of the woòd.

152

THIS IS A SIGN, take it all in all! It was hanging outside the tavern door in Deerfield, New Hampshire, in 1770, and possibly for long before that. The measurements are 1 ft., 5½ in. by 2 ft., 8½ in. It is the property of Dr. J. O. Tilton, of Lexington.

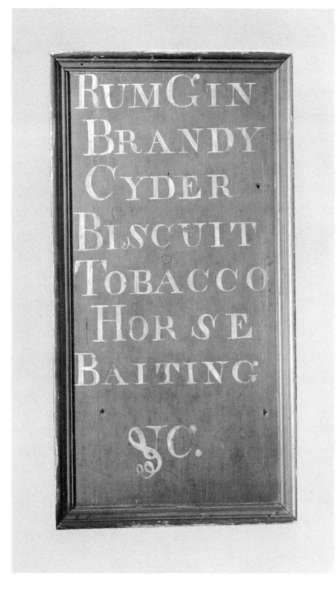

153

THE SIGN that hung outside the Munroe Tavern in Lexington for the one hundred and sixty-three years of its public hospitality, dates from 1695. The original lettering of "Wm. Munro" is faintly traceable through the later paint. From the hands of this first William Munro the property, and consequently the sign, passed through several families, but came back in 1770 to the Munroes again, who by this time had added a final "e" to their name. This is recorded on the sign, for in 1775 it was repainted in the arrangement in which we now see it: "Entertainment" at the top, then a generous punch-bowl 1 ft., 3 in. across, underneath it some decorative leaves, and across the bottom "By Wm. Munroe" grandson of the man whose name he painted over. This sign witnessed, on the 19th of April, 1775, the retreating British under Earl Percy as they "piled the furniture in the bar-room, set it on fire, made targets of the ceiling, and bayonetted on the doorstep John Raymond." The tavern was given up in the year 1858, and the sign taken down. It hangs to-day on the walls of the old barroom, but a few feet from the position it held for so many years. [SEE DRAWING 46.]

154

FROM the old Hartwell Tavern in Lincoln, near the boundaries of both Lexington and Concord, once hung this sign. To-day it may be seen in the Hancock Clarke House in Lexington. The panel is of pine, while the morticed and tenoned framework is, of course, of harder wood, less likely to be pulled apart by north-east gales.

STEPHEN PATCH chose to honor the father of his country by painting his portrait on the signboard that swung before his tavern on Lexington Road, Concord. Washington is in proper uniform—buff trousers, blue coat with gold braid, and black hat with a red plume. Beside him is his horse, and in the rear a camp scene of tents and a flag. On the reverse side is an Indian head.

The sign is very simply mortised together. The posts are turned from $1\frac{1}{2}$ in. square; the top and bottom cross pieces are cut out of $1\frac{1}{4}$ in. stock; the oval picture is 1 in. thick and measures 1 ft., $10\frac{3}{4}$ in. by 2 ft., $8\frac{3}{4}$ in. inside a $\frac{1}{4}$ in. by $1\frac{1}{2}$ in. strip of some such wood as ash, bent around to form a frame. The height over all is 4 ft., $4\frac{1}{2}$ in. Two twisted and wrought iron arms $\frac{5}{8}$ in. square reach up to hold onto a $\frac{3}{4}$ in. round rod above.

Owned by the Antiquarian Society of Concord, Massachusetts, which has a number of valuable signs.

156

THE STORY has it that when, in 1774, this ferocious lion lost favour, along with the King, whose authority he represented, the sign was nailed flat against the tavern, lion innermost, and a punch bowl, over which there could be no dispute, painted on the visible side. Thus were neither patriot nor royalist offended. The sign is considered by its owner, the Concord Antiquarian Society, to be much older than the date of 1797 which was probably painted on it when David Reed had accumulated enough money to have things freshly painted and his initials added. The word "Entertainment" should be a caution to all persons who can draw well formed letters but who are too temperamental (or lazy) to figure out the spacing before they begin! The mouldings are painted, some red, some black, and the lettering is black also. Black and probably yellow-brown were used on the lion, who had a red mouth and tongue. Within the mouldings the decorated panel measures 1 ft., 8½ in. by 2 ft., 2½ in., and is 1⅛ in. thick. Above and below are pieces of the same thickness, but the grain of the wood runs horizontally instead of vertically. Part of the bottom is broken off, and there is something gone from between the points of the broken pediment. The posts are turned with great individuality from 1⅞ in. square. Over all, exclusive of the iron hangers, the sign now measures 2 ft., 6 in. by 3 ft., 6 in., and is 3 in. thick. These iron hangers are 3/16 in. by 1 in., and extend about a foot down along the sides. The rod the sign hung from must have been ¾ in. in diameter.

157

PROBABLY of Long Island origin, but possibly having crossed the Sound from New England, this sign must be entered with some such foreword of caution. We wish we could find out more about the Ship Ahoy Inn which started the century so prosperously. The gentleman on the other side has on a red coat. We wonder whether he is the proprietor or some great personage expected to lend the prestige of his character in return for such a show of homage. Mr. John M. Woolsey, of New York and Petersham, Massachusetts, has the sign at his summer residence.

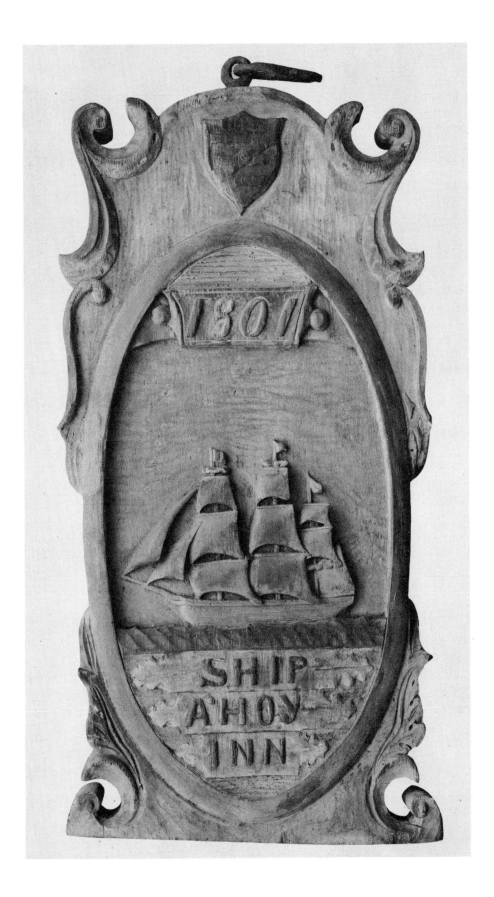

158

THE REVERSE of the sign shown in Plate 157.

159

OF THE astonishingly many things and creatures permitted to fly from the barn tops and point out the way to the wind, the arrow is at once the most logical and the commonest. Nowadays it would invariably be built of metal, but there was a time when wood was elected, as this vane testifies. The arrow itself is 3 ft. long, cut out of a ¾ in. piece of pine. It turns on an iron rod, projecting from a flat pole ¾ in. thick, 3 ft. long, and tapering from 2 in. in width to ⅞ in. at the junction with the arrow. The owner is Mr. E. Gordon Parker.

160

THERE are not as many ship weather vanes as one would expect to find. For them to look like proper ships, too much rigging was required, and the spars were too delicate to hold out with any assurance against the outdoor exposure. But a few sturdy examples are to be found.

The hull of the one illustrated here is just a flat board bevelled slightly at the bow and stern. The rigging is, of course, copper wire. To keep her nose pointed into the wind, this bark has only her mizzen and mizzen gaff sails set, which is quite in accorddance with the best nautical tradition.

161

WE CONCLUDED he was originally a cod, and repainted him accordingly. He is cut from a 1¼ in. board, measures 5½ in. wide and 1 ft., 6 in. over all, which happens to be also on the waterline. If his coloring is wrong, you may blame the encyclopædia.

162

THE HORSE, too, has always been a favorite motif. He is not always in quite so much of a hurry as in this instance. Sometimes he shows his exuberance by stepping very high, or his ancestors by the scornful angle of his head and neck, but we prefer this exhibition of primitive spirits—at least as long as we don't have to ride him. He may have had a saddle once upon a time, for a cinch is just discernible around his middle. Although the paint has sadly faded, his metal eye is cold and clear. He is up in the air again on Mr. Franklin H. Trumbull's wood shed at New Boston, New Hampshire.

It should be noted that in the drawing the staff on which he swings is a reconstruction made as correctly as the evidence permitted. [SEE DRAWING 47.]

163

MORE WEATHERVANES. A flying duck gets rid of his feet tempo-
rarily, so he is all right; but it does seem hard on the poor rooster! They all belong to Mrs. John C. Spring of Boston.

164

THOSE more familiar with the sport tell us that this rooster is a game cock. His feathers were originally black, while his comb and wattles still show a dullish red. His legs were once yellow, like those of all other fowl. As he swings about at the pleasure of the breezes, his terra firma gyrates with him. [SEE DRAWING 48.]

"A WEATHERVANE COCK IN PINE. *American*, 1710-1740

"A boldly modeled bird carved in pine, standing on and attached to a pine ball. The legs, comb, wattles and a part of the tail are iron. It is in the original paint of a dull greenish black hue, the wattles and the comb in red, the ball in greenish blue. It was found in Methuen, Massachusetts, and was probably perched on a church spire. A research is now under way for its pedigree. "*Height, including ball, 40 inches; length, 27 inches; diameter of ball, 10 inches*

"From the Private Collection of Miss Traver."

The above description, together with the illustration, is reproduced from a catalogue of The Anderson Galleries, New York, with their permission.

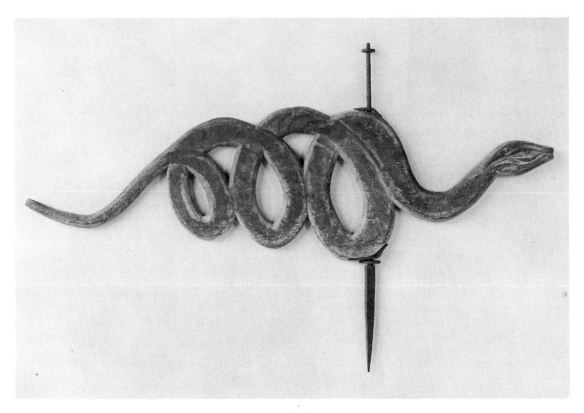

166

JUST the idea of seeing a coiled snake way up over the tree-tops is enough to startle anyone. But here he is, in person, with wicked eye and thrashing tail. There are few vanes to be seen that are his equal. It is no wonder that while the writer was making up his mind about him he should have been purchased in Boston by someone else. More than a year later he turned up in Connecticut. The piece is ⅞ in. thick, 10 in. high, and 3 ft., 1 in. long. (Stretched out, he would measure 8 ft!). His body is about 2½ in. thick at its widest. It is streaked in gray, olive-green, and black, with the underside plain gray. The 7½ in. long spike turns, with a washer, into a 5/16 in. rod 13 in. long, on which the figure rotates.

167

DRAGONS were more common in the old days than they are now. This one is having a battle with a snake, which he has bitten so successfully that it has had to be repaired with four screws and a strip of tin. He is a slate colour, with a black delineation of his scales. The over-all measurements are 1 ft., 1 in., by 1 ft., 6½ in., by ⅝ in.

12. MIRRORS

THE GENERAL NAME OF MIRROR and the more specific name of looking-glass bring up graphically the advancement from polished metal surfaces to the far more satisfactory tin- or silver-backed glasses of relatively modern times.

As a matter of fact, both types of reflecting surfaces can be traced back into the Greek, Roman, and even Chinese civilizations; but glass mirrors never really came into their own until Venice, at the beginning of the Sixteenth Century, began their manufacture as a commercial enterprise. For nearly a century and a half, thanks to the jealous way in which they guarded their secrets, they held what amounted to a monopoly of the trade, making the polished metal mirrors appear relics of a time gone by.

Eventually, of course, in spite of drastic laws, threatening even the penalty of death for any Venetian glassmaker who carried his secrets beyond the borders of his own state, England, and France too, learned how to make the article that was in such demand. For we find that in 1676 "looking glasses far larger and better than any that come from Venice" were seen by John Evelyn on his visit to the Duke of Buckingham's glass works at Lambeth, England.

Here in the New England Colonies we were dependent upon European glass, exclusively, for many years. Whether or not it is possible to tell Venetian mirror glass from that made in England, the writer cannot say. A bevel was put on the glass in each locality. It was a soft-edged bevel, and flat, for it was worked on by hand, falling off not more than four or five degrees from the main surface of the glass.

The date when the New England Colonies first began to supply their own needs for mirrors may be located quite definitely by the following plaintive advertisement in the Boston *News Letter* of November 12, 1767:

"Said Whiting does more at present towards manufacturing Looking-Glasses than any one in the Province, or perhaps on the Continent, and would be glad of Encouragement enough to think it worth while to live."

It should be emphasized, however, that from the earliest times up to the present we have always imported mirrors—from Italy, England, Holland, France, Spain, China, or wherever else our fancy has happened, at the time, to turn. In this discussion, therefore, we are quite aware that it is a cosmopolitan family whose history we are tracing.

In the early years, when the actual glass was so precious, it is quite natural that the mediæval fashion of hand mirrors should be continued or revived for a while in this country, with the difference that glass was now used instead of polished metal. Such would probably be the low-priced looking-glasses mentioned in the inventories during the first half of the Seventeenth Century.

The typical late Seventeenth Century mirror is small and squaresh, or nearly square. The frame is of some such handsome wood as walnut, solid or veneered on a pine base; or it was frequently just pine. In its finest form the moulding is unmistakable, with a small half-round toward the outside, and a larger bolection swelling generously forward to hold the glass considerably to the front. There is usually a high top, or cresting, variously decorated, and held in place by vertical braces that are cut into the rear of the top moulding. The attractive backward curve that this top customarily takes is not intentional. It comes as the woods shrink, the thick horizontal grain of the pine back pulling against the thin vertical veneer.

Attached at the base there was occasionally a brass arm holding a candle out where its flame would be reflected cheerfully in the glass background. Such lighting, and the mere use of plenty of wall mirrors, brightened up the dark walls and gave one a sense of space where it did not really exist.

If we feel that we should give a name to this small and square type, "William and Mary" will serve the purpose. Their reign in England, lasting as it did from 1689 to 1702, covers the years when the type prevailed. As a matter of fact, mirrors of this proportion and of similar design were made for many years afterward, but a new design then had come into favour.

The first thing we notice about the early Eighteenth Century mirror is the shape. It is tall and narrow. Seventeenth Century glasses had been more or less square, because there was no reason for making them otherwise. They were considered as framed pictures. The proportions changed when their ambitions outgrew the limits of a single sheet of glass. One sheet was simply set above another, upper overlapping lower, the rebate in the frame being wedged especially to receive the curious combination. At the same time the moulding flattened in section and, with its greater vertical length, appeared much lighter. At the head and for a short distance down the sides it broke, together with the bevel on the glass, into a series of extremely slight curves and offsets. We can see this same outline on the backs of Queen Anne chairs, and in the panelling of the doors of cabinet-topped scrutoirs of the same period. The cresting, too, ran over onto the sides and was even reflected in a skirt at the bottom, until the outline of the frame was entirely secondary to what surrounded it. Brass attachments for candles were more common than in the century previous.

The first steps in this development produced work that is usually given the name of Queen Anne. She reigned only from 1702 to 1714, but the period ascribed to her in the history of furniture should be more generously bounded. After this, as the style elaborates, it may be classified as Georgian, with sub-headings indicating the influence of the various distinguished cabinetmakers, such as Chippendale, Hepplewhite, and Sheraton, who dominated the scene.

Among the many influences that were at play, such as those of Italy, and Holland by way of England, there are also the styles of the Orient to be considered. As early as the last quarter of the Seventeenth Century English schoolgirls were being taught the art of japanning, much as they have music lessons to-day; and lacquered furniture "in the Oriental taste" continued to be made up to the middle of the Eighteenth Century. It was an unnatural fashion, and like all fads was subjected to much ridicule in the literature of the day. To this interest in things of the Far East, however, then known as "Indian," we are probably indebted for the "Chinese" courting mirrors. Fragile, beautiful, exotic, (for there is every indication that they were imported) they were much in favour during the years just preceding the Revolutionary War.

There are two common types that we have not yet mentioned. One of these is the round convex mirror that was hung, entirely for decorative effect, on the more formal walls during the last quarter of the Eighteenth Century. The other is a horizontal mirror designed especially to be placed above the opening of a fireplace. The mantel mirror, coming into fashion in England during the reign of William and Mary, may be seen here in the Queen Anne period and in each successive style thereafter. At first it had a simple frame holding three sheets of bevelled glass, the outer two overlapping the center one. In the middle of the century it became more ornate (the Chippendale mirror in the Marmion Room of the American Wing of the Metropolitan Museum is a remarkable example), and when finally the classic forms held sway, the mantel mirror took on its cornice and its columns and was eventually incorporated in the panelling of the room.

As the Nineteenth Century rumbled into position most of the graceful freehand curves were pushed aside to make way for the triumphal entry of the Roman orders, which had up to this time been merely occasional visitors. In mirrors the flat cornice is all important, and the frame is squared-up with half-columns flanking the two glass panels, now divided by a narrow strip of wood.

The decoration of the glass itself began with the "diamond cut" pattern that was often put on the upper glass of a mirror of the Queen Anne type—for the upper glass was not intended to be used. It was, like a drum major's hat, merely an aid to dignity.

After the Queen Anne period the idea of decorating the glass is dropped, to be revived toward the close of the century with increased enthusiasm. Starting timidly with conventional designs, this time painted on the back face of the glass, the art developed rapidly and was ready to commemorate the naval victories of the War of 1812 on both mirrors and clocks of the period.

But how much has our material, pine, to do with all this development? Really a great deal. In the Seventeenth Century, as we have already pointed out, and during the Queen Anne period as well, the most usual thing was to use a veneer of walnut on a pine backing. A great many frames, however, were made entirely of pine. Sometimes the pine was painted black and decorated in gold.

This situation prevailed until about 1750 when, with a very gradual transition, mahogany took the place of walnut, used either in a solid board or in veneer on pine. Carved surfaces now were picked out in gold, and sometimes the whole frame was covered with it. As the trick was acquired of making out of a composition the parts that had at first been carved, the gold was needed all the more. By the beginning of the Nineteenth Century, in the majority of cases, one does not see the wood at all. The glass, no longer bevelled, is held within an entirely painted and gilded design. But the structural parts, the thin backing of the glass, and the base under the plaster and gold ornament, were more probably than not still made of pine.

168

WE CAN GET a vivid impression of the value of mirror glass at a time when a little broken piece like this was utilized in this way. It is a hand glass, about 7 or 8 in. long. Mr. A. G. Baldini was the owner at the time this photograph was taken.

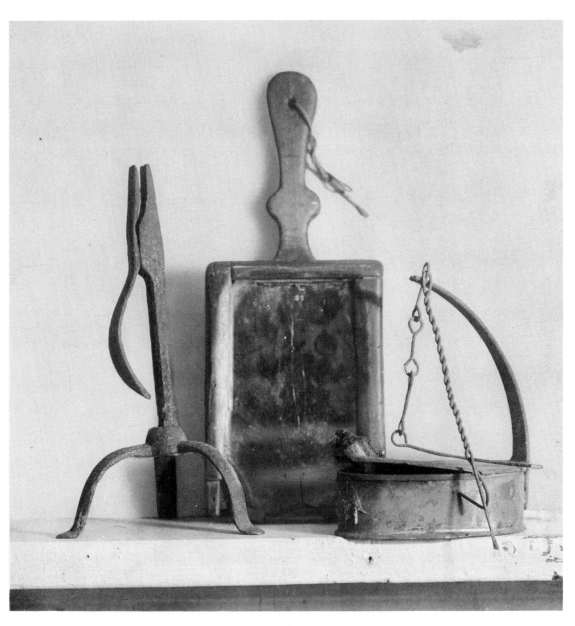

169

A RUSHLIGHT HOLDER, a hand mirror, and a betty lamp are shown on a ledge in the witch house at Rockport, Massachusetts. No one has found a reasonable solution of the problem of how to restore the head of the mirror, so we have left it untouched and drawn attention elsewhere. Mr. Oliver E. Williams owns the two lights and the writer the mirror.

170

WHEN you see a mirror framed with a moulding of this detail—
the outside low with a little bead, then a generous swelling forward to cover the rebate that holds the glass—you may be fairly
certain that you have something interesting, fashioned in the
late Seventeenth or early Eighteenth Century. You must not
expect to appear particularly handsome in one of these early
glasses.

This mirror measures 6¼ in. by 7¼ in. outside; the moulding is
run from a ¾ in. piece 1⅜ in. wide. It came from Vermont with
the mirror shown in Plate 171.

 171

THIS MIRROR was found in Brattleboro, Vt., in the same shop as
the more elaborate one shown in Plate 170. As both are very
nearly of the same size, and both stained red, it is reasonable to
suppose that this one was made, though at a later date, to go
with the other. [SEE DRAWING 49.]

172

STANDING MIRRORS of this kind are not often run across. This one is noteworthy in that it is wider àt the bottom than at the top. Whether this was intentional or merely the result of careless manufacture, might be disputed at some length, but the writer inclines to the first theory. It is too well made to justify the suspicion that the maker was a full quarter of an inch out of the way. The back support is made of oak, swinging from iron staples, while the frame proper is pine, painted first in a coat of black, then streak-daubed with grey, probably to simulate marble. The over all height is 10½ in., the width 6¼ in. at the top, 6½ in. at the bottom, and the moulding run from a ¾ in. to 1¼ in. strip.

173

ANOTHER very early mirror, said to have been for several generations at least in the neighbourhood of Boston. The carving, especially in the little crow's-feet near the top, is quite like that on the spoon rack at the Wayside Inn (Plate 122). At the very top of the design there was originally a projection of some sort which has been broken off. The moulding around the glass is painted red, while the rest of the visible woodwork is black. The conventionalized leaf carving is as deep as 3/16 in.

174

A VENEERED William and Mary mirror, with its original bevelled glass and its cresting still in place, is one of the finest sights
that the realm of furniture can offer. In this case the veneering
is done in walnut over pine, the grains of the two woods running
at right angles to each other. In addition to the small outside
bead and the larger convex profile, such as the mirrors just described and illustrated have, there is in this example a trim little
moulding next to the glass. This adds a great deal of dignity.
The origin of this mirror is believed to be English, but from the
point of view of this book it is an American mirror, having been
naturalized here many, many years ago. It is in the Boston
Museum of Fine Arts.

There are two heavy and elaborated mirrors of this type in the
Château of Assez-le-Rideau that stand almost in a class by themselves. There is another fine one at the Victoria and Albert
Museum. With Italy still the recognized leader in the production of looking-glasses at this time, there is every reason to expect this uniformity of style in the several countries.

175

EXCEPT for the loss of its cresting, this William and Mary mirror is in perfect condition. It is mahogany veneer on a heavy pine base which is made up of three strips. First there is a frame of ⅝ in. by 2⅝ in. wood halved at the corners. Next comes a thin strip, ¼ in. by 1 in. standing on end flush with the back of the frame just mentioned. Finally, making the hypotenuse of the right triangle rests the third piece of pine. It also measures ⅝ in. by 2⅝ in., but is bevelled and rebated underneath, and rounded on top to receive the 3/64 in. mahogany veneer. Around the outside, on a little platform that has been left, is put the ¼ in. by ½ in. half-round mahogany moulding. Every joint, originally, was merely glued. In the top board of the frame are the two dovetailed cuts from which once ran braces to keep the veneered cresting from warping (which it always did to some extent in spite of them). In the middle of this same top board across the lower edge are two diagonal holes with a cord through them to hang the mirror by. The glass is 1 ft., 1⅝ in. by 1 ft., 4¾ in., actual measurement, about ⅛ in. thick, and has a ⅞ in. broad flat bevel. Scratched boldly across the lower half is the name "Edward." It makes one think of a small window light in Williamsburg, Virginia, where there is cut the startling exclamation, "Oh, fatal day!"

The little rooster in the picture knows just as much about these things as anybody else. He is a gilded metal weather vane, 9¼ in. high.

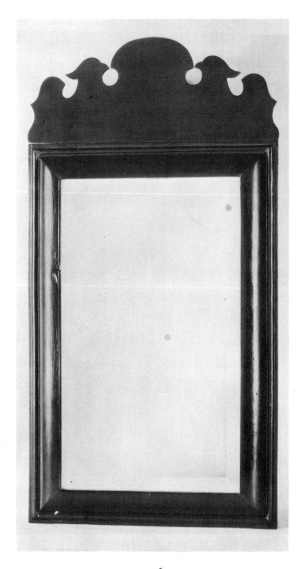

176

WHILE the more elaborate mirrors such as this one were usually made of rarer woods over a backing of pine, here we have one made of pine alone. The bevel, which is one of the characteristics of a piece of early glass, is just discernible at the lower edge. The measurements are 21¾ in. high by 11½ in. wide. The frame itself is 1⅝ in. in width.

As interesting evidence of the rarity and value of looking-glasses in the early seventeen hundreds we can see the price, appearing on the back of this mirror, of £3/10. Considering the much greater value of the pound in those days, the cost of this mirror of Mr. Henry W. Erving's is astounding.

177

IT IS a pretty rash thing to give a date to any of these home-
made all-pine mirrors, for the farther away from the cabinetmaker you get, the less distinguishable are the lines and dates of
style. The first half of the Eighteenth Century, however, should
be an accurate though widely limited dating of this mirror.

The earthenware light in front of it operates like a betty lamp,
but is set up in the manner of a candlestick. The upper portion
is in no wise different from the little Roman lamps, two thousand or so years old. Mr. Oliver E. Williams owns the pieces in
this group. [SEE DRAWING 50.]

178

THE TOP and bottom profiles give this extremely simple mirror an astonishing amount of style. At one time it was painted grey, but this must have taken away much of its beauty. The glass, measuring 8¼ in. by 10½ in., is held in place by little metal wedges, driven sidewise into the single piece of ⅞ in. pine of which the mirror back and frame is made. It came from Laconia, New Hampshire.

FOR THIS unusual piece we will have to make up a name that will be properly descriptive. Perhaps Tall Man-Short Man Mirror best tells the story, for by the different slants of the two faces both sizes of men can be accommodated. Each 4 in. by 8 in. glass is held by a 1 in. wide moulding, and the whole set upon a ¾ in. back board measuring 10¾ in. wide by 13¾ in. tall. The mirrors stand out about 2 in. from this back piece at their intersection with each other. The mirror came from near Fitchburg and is now owned by Mr. Henry D. Sleeper, of East Gloucester, Massachusetts.

180

IN THESE TWO PIER GLASSES we see all of the characteristics of the Queen Anne period. The square proportions of William and Mary mirrors have given way to these excessive heights, with the glass in two sections, upper overlapping lower, as one of the examples happens to show. The moulding of the frame is a different shape, too, and the straight lines of the sides and top are broken with slight offsets and curves around the upper third. Mitring the upper corners is no longer possible, nor is it now possible to apply the veneer in thin sheets dampened, glued, and pressed down with sand bags. The new surfaces are too complicated to permit such methods. Pine still usually served as a base, but it was not moulded. The richer wood, generally walnut, was glued flat upon the pine and the moulded profile worked by hand upon it. The same irregular and beautiful outline was given to the glass and its hand-worked bevel.

The left-hand example is in the Metropolitan Museum collection. It is all pine, decorated in gold on a black background, and measures 1 ft., 8 in. by 5 ft., 4¼ in. The date is given as 1700-1725.

On the right is a mirror in the new wing at the Boston Museum of Fine Arts.

181

THE DESIGN at the head of this pier glass was planned with reference to two minor axes, each running at 45° up into a corner. An "S" curve, or cyma, on either side of each axis softens the angles of the corners and makes the rather unusual little point that accents the center of the top. Over all measurements are 1 ft., 4½ in. by 3 ft. The moulding is walnut, 1½ in. wide and ⅜ in. thick, veneered with the grain running crosswise onto a pine base, as shows in the lower left-hand corner. As no moulding plane was known in those days that could be run around the curves at the head, the work had to be done by hand, with a result that was vibrant with minor irregularities. The bevel of the upper section of glass follows the curving of the frame and overlaps the lower section, all according to custom. The owner is Mr. Alfred Uhler, of Concord, Massachusetts, who purchased it near Concord from a family in whose possession it had evidently been for many generations.

182

THE FANCIFUL TOP on this beautiful little mirror (it measures but 9½ in. by 11½ in.) places it definitely in the same period as the more elaborate pier glasses of the early Seventeen Hundreds. The frame is a thin veneering ⅞ in. wide, on a moulded pine base. It is in this sort of work that the veneer was pressed into shape and held in position, while the glue hardened, by heavy sand bags. But as the outline of mirrors grew more complicated it became increasingly difficult to make the flat sheet of veneer conform to the warped surface beneath it. The solution, as we have already explained, lay in keeping the base flat, however much it might curve around in outline. On this a relatively thick moulded veneer could easily be applied. Thus the pine base gave strength and generally determined the silhouette, while the veneer was responsible for all the surface beauty. This minute looking glass is owned by Mrs. Alfred Uhler, of Concord, Massachusetts.

183

THE BEVEL on all early mirror glass is so very slight that it is seldom that it shows in a photograph. This mirror has its original hand bevelled glass and the frame is lacquered in black and gold. Mr. Alfred Uhler, of Concord, is the owner.

When the backing is sufficiently cracked and dulled, an old mirror becomes quite like a beautiful picture on the wall, and then more than ever the outlines and contours and textures are what we look at.

184

IN A MODEST WAY this mirror proclaims its Queen Anne date just as surely as did the more pretentious pier glasses. The moulding is similar in shape, and the walnut veneering is done in heavy pieces, moulded by hand, with the corners turned without mitring. Joints in the wood came just beyond the corners. Above the frame is a cresting, but quite different in design from any seen in the William and Mary mirrors. Most characteristic is the suggestion of the broken pediment which, from the first quarter of the Eighteenth Century on, was usually the dominating motif at the upper corners.

On the table are a very simple betty lamp and a niddy-noddy, or hand-reel. These reels, like many of the smaller mirrors, were often made by young blades for their best girls. The writer found one once that had two hearts with a piercing arrow carved upon the handle. Mirrors made under these circumstances are spoken of as courting mirrors, a term sometimes applied in a general way to all mirrors about a foot square.

185

THIS MIRROR is remarkably like the one in Plate 184. It brings up two interesting points. The first is the use of gilded plaster ornament in a decorated strip on the side of the frame and in the centre of the cresting. The plaster was spread over the wood in a layer no thicker than was absolutely necessary to cover the irregularities in the grain or to receive the modelling. On an un-moulded surface it would be no more than half again as thick as a postcard. When gilded the surface could be made as smooth as gold itself. The second point is not noticeable in the photograph, but is worth discussion. At the back of the cresting there is a single brace running up behind the shell ornament. This part is quite straight. But the two arms of the broken pediment, not being braced, have curled backward a very appreciable distance. The thin vertical veneering could not hold against the shrinking of the thicker horizontal pine backing. In this one mirror, then, is to be seen the answer to the question of whether the backward curve of an old cresting is accidental or intentional.

186

THIS MIRROR and the two preceding it were collected at different times and from different states, yet they seem to go together like a, b, and c. How inevitable it was that the scalloping of the top should be pushed over the sides and even find its way across the bottom. It should be understood that this is a very small and plain example of the period. The more typical glasses of this time were still of pier glass proportions and richly ornamented. This looking glass should be compared with the much later one of mahogany, illustrated in Plate 203. There was a curious restoration to public favour of this design with only slight modifications. The glass of this mirror measures 7½ in. by 11¾ in. Below the mirror is a miniature six-board pine chest, 5 in. tall, and a little keg big enough to hold a noonday supply of water (or rum).

187

AN INTERESTING adaptation of the design just shown is this triangular looking-glass, constructed of pine and at one time stained red in imitation of mahogany. It is very nicely cut out and put together, except at one point,—the cresting rests perceptibly over to the left of the centre of the glass. The over all dimensions are 1 ft., 2⅛ in. by 1 ft., 9¾ in., and the wood throughout 7/16 in. thick. The glass, within a 1¼ in. wide frame, is a triangle 1 ft., 4 in. wide at the base and 8¼ in. in altitude. Whether we consider this design successful or not, we must admire the originality of the man who made the attempt. "Interesting things," says a very wise friend of the writer's, "come from interesting people!"

188

THESE two looking-glasses seem to show what all the earlier designs have been working toward. And at the same time you can see in the left-hand example how, with architecture dominating the design of the cresting, the introduction of supporting columns was foreshadowed. Dating 1790-1800, they are, almost as a matter of course, mahogany on pine. In the Metropolitan Museum.

189

THE TENDENCY toward freedom and grace that underlay the development of mirrors received its greatest, and in a way its final assistance from the guidance of Thomas Chippendale. The period of his influence is, roughly, from 1750 to 1775. English designers were already interested in the three sources—Louis XV, Chinese, and Gothic—from which he drew his inspiration, but it was his ability that took these faddish and widely different styles, adapted them, and combined them into something entirely his own and thoroughly homogeneous. It must not be thought that he was without his critics. No less a personage than the Surveyor to the King was undoubtedly aiming at Chippendale when he deplored seeing "an unmeaning scrawl of C's inverted and looped together, taking the place of Greek and Roman elegance even in our most expensive decorations. It is called French, and let them have the praise of it!" Yet the master designer, though frequently attacked, seems always to have held the upper hand.

We can see and admire these "C" scrolls that have "taken the place of Greek and Roman elegance" in this little gilt mirror, made at a time when Chippendale's factory was influencing all of England and to a large extent the Colonies as well. We see, furthermore, the freedom, the absence of rigid symmetry, that are characteristics of the period. The mirror is probably of English manufacture. The wood is hard pine, with over all dimensions of 1 ft. by 2 ft., 4 in. Inside the 1⅛ in. frame the glass measures 7¼ in. by 12⅞ in. Some of the ornaments such as the blossoms and the projecting leaf ends are applied, for the carved board making the cresting is but an inch thick, and in places the design is built up to a thickness of 2⅜ in. The front of the frame is gilded over a thin coat of plaster, bright upon the rectangular frame, while on the carving it is dull and has a reddish tone. The back and sides are painted yellow so that such parts as might by chance be seen shall not give away the fact that they were slighted!

190

MANTEL MIRRORS were occasionally in use during those years of artistic wisdom when there were no shelves to be crowded with inconsequential ornaments over the all-important fireplaces. Instead, there was usually just a simple panel, on which there might be hung a mirror, sometimes designed especially for that position. The problem of excessive length was solved, as in the case·of the pier glasses, by making the glass quite frankly in more than one section—in the case of mantel mirrors, in three. The writer ventures the statement that nowhere is there a more beautiful mantel mirror than this example of Chippendale style, now in the Marmion Room of the American Wing of the Metropolitan Museum. Perhaps it has never had any connection with New England. Of that we cannot say; but as practically all of the splendid examples of Chippendale type, all up and down the Colonies, were imported from England, we have decided to use it as an illustration here.

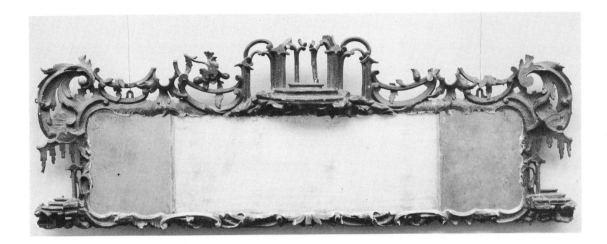

191

THIS is a small "Chinese" courting mirror once owned by the writer. It could not have measured more than 6 or 7 in. in width. The painting is on the back of the glass and must be done in an awkward order, for first on go the veins of a leaf, then the leaf over them, and lastly the background painted over everything. The accepted theory is that mirrors such as this were brought back from China in the trading vessels. A pencil note on the back, if authentic, checks perfectly with the opinion that these mirrors were popular about 1770, for it states that the piece was brought into the country by Wesley Burnham in 1771.

192

PROPERLY, this kind of a "Chinese" courting mirror should be hung up in its original box, but the boxes have seldom been preserved. In the more elaborate ones the glass itself is cut with a few delicate decorations that show a frosted white along the edges of the reflecting surface.

The painted lines in this glass border, in spite of their simplicity, are beautiful. The ever changing outline is very cleverly built up from the even rectangle. Although there is a hundred years between the 1770 mirror and the 1670 house (1663, to be exact), the shadow-moulded boarding makes an agreeable background.

193

HERE is a "Chinese" Courting mirror hung properly; only most of us are not fortunate enough to have the original box to use. The wooden pegs that hold the mirror in place are visible in the photograph. The dimensions, over all, are 1 ft., 4¼ in. by 11¾ in. Mrs. Samuel Dale Stevens, of North Andover, Massachusetts is the owner.

It will be noticed that in all of the courting mirrors here illustrated, the decorations are based on leaves and flowers, or are simply geometrical designs. Any idea of painting a real scene or a portrait upon glass did not appear until the end of the century.

194

NOT ALL of these "Chinese" courting mirrors were originally boxed. Some of them may be found provided with a solid pine back, about a half an inch thick, finished off with a thumbnail moulding that followed the irregular pattern of the more delicate inner mouldings.

As an example of this less fragile sort we present this one from the collection in the Metropolitan Museum.

195

IN STILL more elaborate designs we may find the head embellished with a frame and cresting of veneered woods quite as much in keeping with New England's furniture traditions as the rest of the mirror is out of keeping with them. It almost seems as if this mysterious country, wherever it may have been, had begun to be interested in the other man's civilization or was catering to his trade.

This example of this type, measures, over all, 10 in. by 1 ft., 4½ in. The reflecting surface is 5 ¾ in. by 8 in. About it is the usual band of painted glass, in this case a rich wavy striping of greens and browns, and about that the veneering of alternating pieces, 3/32 in. thick, of light and dark wood. From the collection of Mr. F. J. Finnerty, of Boston and Haverhill.

196

WE CAN only guess about this mirror. May we not wonder if some man had seen a "Chinese" courting mirror and tried to fashion one very simply for himself? The moulding might have been given him; the picture, which is painted upon glass, he might have done himself. The fact that a house and not a floral design was chosen as the subject tends to date this several years later than the mirrors that we believe inspired it. Mr. Frederick R. Child, Jr., of Concord, Massachusetts, is the owner.

197

THERE is another sort of looking-glass that we have come to associate with the return voyages of our Eighteenth Century traders. Though not of a uniform pattern, as are the "Chinese" courting mirrors, they all bear what we may speak of as a family resemblance to one another, and show a last faint echo of the style of Chippendale. They are certainly not exquisite in workmanship, probably not being intended to find their way into the very finest houses. There is, therefore, some danger of giving them an earlier date than that which is rightfully theirs.

The two illustrated here are dated 1790-1800. That on the left is gilt; that on the right has been painted brown, and measures, over all, 9¾ in. by 18¼ in. The picture is painted on glass. Both pieces are in the Metropolitan Museum.

198

ANOTHER of these imported looking glasses, which is practically the same size and of the same moulding section as the two shown in Fig. 201. The scrolls, the bird, the flowers, are very crudely done. Although there are unmistakable sparkles of gilt in a few places, the greater part of the mirror was apparently painted. The frame is still a cream color with a pattern in darker colors repeated on it. This mirror is shown hanging on a wall of shadow-moulded boarding in the Browne House at Watertown, Massachusetts.

199

INASMUCH as so many of the mirrors in the Colonies were of European manufacture, we do not hesitate to show this naïve example, for although it is quite unlike anything that we think of as being early American, the evidence goes to show that it is no recent importation. Mr. Lockwood, in his book, illustrates a very similar looking-glass which was brought to this country from the West Indies in the last quarter of the Eighteenth Century. Both frame and cresting are made of glass, cut on the under side and silvered. The edges are bound with paper and glued to the pine framework. Cut crudely into the back of the cresting is a heart enclosing the initials P.F. It is curious that anything with as much artistic workmanship as this should be so crookedly arranged at the top. To cut glass along any but straight lines seems to have presented almost insurmountable difficulties. The over all measurements are 10½ in. by 1 ft., 10¾ in., the glass rectangle within the frame, 8 in. by 10¼ in; and the pine backing ⅝ in. thick.

200

CONVEX MIRRORS are to be found in all sizes, from that of this piece of which the glass is 5½ in. in diameter, to about 1 ft., 8½ in., which is the diameter of the mirror in Fig. 205. They date from the last quarter of the Eighteenth Century, some of them even being made in the early Nineteenth. After nearly a century and a half of use, the gilded plaster coating is invariably cracking off at one place or another, so that the thinness of the surfacing may be examined. The circle of wood was glued up in various ways, as the cracks indicate.

On the ledge is an old silhouette in a gold frame, a tin savings bank of several years ago, and a metal mould in which were once made the composition ornaments that one sees so often on the tops of mahogany mirrors. The ledge itself is interesting as being all the shelf that there was over the huge oak beam that spanned a Seventeenth Century fireplace. (Often there was none at all.) During the first half of the next century even this occasional ledge disappeared, only to return in the wider proportions that have been retained up to to-day. There is a discrepancy, therefore, of at least a century, between the mirror and its background.

201

CONVEX MIRRORS are sometimes spoken of as girandoles. If they are fitted to hold candles, as is this one, the term is, perhaps, not incorrectly applied, but it should be known that a girandole is technically a cluster of branching lights. The distinction is clearly drawn in *The Ring and the Book:*

> " 'Neath waxlight in a glorified saloon
> Where mirrors multiply the girandole."

From the eagle to the bottom tip of foliage this mirror measures nearly 5 ft. Bird, rocks, foliage, all are carved first in pine, and later surfaced with the thin layer of plaster and gilded. In the twisted ring alternate strands are dull and highly polished, and on other surfaces certain parts, like the eagle's beak, have been picked out to shine above the rest.

This mirror seems to have been in the writer's family since the days when convex mirrors were first popular. About the year 1816 it probably hung in the Adams-Kettell house on Bunker Hill, Charlestown, built in 1790, but in recent years torn down. A formal piece of furniture such as this requires a high ceiling and a large room to be shown to proper advantage.

202

PIER GLASSES continued to be popular, but the frame took on a different character entirely. The glass was still often in two pieces, but no longer did they overlap. There was a dividing strip of wood that soon was separating the mirror below from a picture painted on glass above.

This mirror is 2 ft., 4½ in. wide and 3 ft., 11 in. tall. Its heaviness and formality are in exactly the style of the convex mirror shown in Plate 201, and it has the same family history. In construction it is extremely simple. There is a rebated frame, mitred at the corners, against which are held the blocks and turnings, by screws with the assistance of glue.

203

IN THE first quarter of the Eighteenth Century little mirrors of this sort must have been turned out by the hundreds upon hundreds. The glass was by this time not expensive, the amount of mahogany required for one was very small indeed, and the labour slight.

The construction is built up about a simple frame of pine, ½ in. wide and ⅝ in. thick, slot-mortised at the corners. On the front of this is glued the flat moulded mahogany frame whose corners meet in a mitre. The wood is ⅛ in. by ¾ in. and being placed flush with the outside of the pine projects ¼ in. inside of it to make the rebate for the glass. Against the outside are glued the top, bottom, and four little side scrolls of 3/16 in. mahogany. These glue joints are reinforced by eight blocks of pine, ¼ in. by ¼ in. by 1½ in., glued at intervals into the angle at the back. This particular mirror measures, over all, 11¼ in. by 1 ft., 6¼ in., the glass showing as 9⅝ in. by 7¾ in. The writer bought it at a farm in Carlisle, Massachusetts. The top and three of the side scallops were gone, but have been accurately restored, after the pattern of a mirror that was otherwise like this one, line for line.

204

AMONG the many things that this mirror reflects is the change in style, both in architecture and furniture, that came over this country at the close of the Eighteenth Century. Proportions became more refined, more slender, and mouldings became more delicate, owing, in New England, very largely to the leadership of Samuel McIntire, who himself was not ignorant of the new spirit radiating from the work in England of the brothers Adam. The thin and widely projecting cornice, the delicate applied spiral twisting up the sides, the painting on the back of the upper glass—all of these things were new in furniture. New England society had travelled a long way up the road since the days of little hand mirrors with Italian glass, as the base of the construction of this mirror is a pine frame slot-mortised at the corners. The decoration is built up around it. Little blocks of pine, 1½ in. long and triangular in section, are wedged down around each of the two pieces of glass and glued to the sides of the rebate, so that the glass can neither fall back nor slip sidewise. The gilding is done over the usual plaster sizing. Unfortunately, but as is frequently the case, the painted picture is beginning to work away from the glass. The size, over all, is 1 ft., 2½ in. by 2 ft.

205

WE CONCLUDE the chapter by showing two early Nineteenth Century mirrors from the collection of the Metropolitan Museum. The one on the right dates itself pretty definitely by the painting of a naval battle with the British in the War of 1812. We are sometimes told that these mirrors often had thirteen gold balls in the cornice, one for each of the original thirteen States. Of course, this is tommyrot. You might just as well look around for a chest with thirteen drawer pulls, or a coat with thirteen buttons, and start your story there. The balls were spaced to look right, and numbered what they happened to.

13. LIGHTS

IN ADDITION to the many mirrors that were fitted with brasses to hold candles, there was a large assortment of devices made either to serve as stands for candlesticks and lamps or to hold the candles directly.

First of these, because they were really but miniature mirrors, we mention the sconces. Usually there is a piece of looking-glass within the frame, but in a few beautiful instances the light of the candle is reflected from a sparkling pattern of quill-work, arranged in a shallow box behind the glass face. Quillwork is much in the mood of an old-fashioned valentine. A design of flowers, set in a conventionalized vase, was made from bits of coloured paper rolled tightly into tapers and then cut and twisted ingeniously to make the petals and leaves required by the picture. Silver wire was used, and wax, and a sprinkling of fine grains of coloured glass, until the box shone and sparkled like a Christmas tree. Quillwork, as well as featherwork, painting upon glass, and japanning, were taught by a Mrs. Hiller, at her boarding school for young ladies in Boston, between the years 1748 and 1756—for she so advertised in the local papers.

Occasionally we find a little hanging candle shelf, sometimes backed with a piece of mirror-glass which designates its use beyond a doubt. Such a shelf was easy to move from one wall to another, or it could be set upon a chest of drawers or table.

The lights thus far mentioned took care of what general illumination a house might require. For more specific purposes, such as reading or working, a great array of ingenious portable stands were devised. The candle stands of fixed heights have already been discussed in the chapter on tables, but there are three adjustable stands that should be noted here.

The first is the screw post stand. A cross-arm holding the candles raises or lowers itself on the long central thread, as may the shelf, too, if there is one.

Then there is the wedge post stand, operating in much the same way except that the adjustable parts move freely up and down until set by a wedge pushed in place from above.

The third type is called a ratchet stand. Its operation is similar to that of the other two types.

Sometimes the tops and arms of these stands held the candles themselves in tin or wooden sockets; at other times they ended in a mere bordered platform, and the candle, in a candlestick, was set upon them. The bases, too, were variously constructed. The post might run into a single heavy chunk of wood, or into two halved trestle feet, or into a horizontal board from which extended three or four short legs, or omitting the horizontal board, three legs might come directly from the post.

The ceiling, too, had its share of designs. There were hanging ratchets that could be swung from a summer beam in the middle of the room, to hold betty lamps or candles. There were also, of course, lanterns, whose outstanding advantage was that they were a safe light both out of doors and in. And lastly there are a few examples of chandeliers, veritable bushes of light, that required a high ceiling if they were to be appropriate and safe.

As regards the wood of which this large assortment was constructed, we can say that examples of nearly each sort can be found in pine. Turnings were seldom attempted in soft pine, but everything else, even the extremely delicate ratchets, were often made from it. The argument in its favour, of course, was that the stands and holders thus made were conveniently light to carry about.

One should not forget, however, that the part played by the metals in the development of lighting equipment, though a minor one at first, increased in importance as the era of candles passed.

It is interesting to note in this book that the history of illumination in New England started with the burning of a knot of pine. It was a poor light, however, and welcome only where candles could not be afforded for everyday use.

Candles were for the most part of tallow, either dipped or made in moulds. Dipped candles were irregular in shape, but those that were moulded could be made either plain or fluted. They were also made of bayberry wax and such were procurable "large and small, plain and flowered," as advertised in the Boston *Gazette* of February 20, 1753.

But a new and better form of candle, that made from spermaceti, was already seeking the favour which it shortly was to receive. In the Boston *News-Letter* of March 30, 1748, James Clemens advertised to be sold "Sperma Ceti Candles, exceeding all others for Beauty, Sweetness of Scent when extinguished; Duration, being more than double Tallow Candles of equal size; Dimensions of Flame, nearly four Times more, emitting a soft easy expanding Light, bringing the Object close to the Sight, rather than causing the Eye to trace after them, as all Tallow-Candles do, from a constant Dimness which they produce.—One of these Candles serves the Use and Purpose of Three Tallow Ones, and upon the whole are much pleasanter and cheaper."

Contemporaneous with the early candles there were rushlights and the betty lamps. The former was but a stem peeled down and dipped in hot tallow. The betty lamp was scarcely more brilliant. Originally Dutch, imported, and of rather minute workmanship, it consisted of an iron or brass box for fat or oil with a spout leading out of it for a round wick of twisted cotton. It hung by its slender hook or rested flat.

"Newburyport bettys" were made at the town of that name in Massachusetts from 1680. It is not unreasonable to suppose that soon after that date new and more natural patterns were being experimented with to take the place of the exotic design. Metal and glass lamps burning whale oil were evolved, and near the end of the Seventeenth Century the advantages of a wide flat wick were discovered. More important still was the discovery, about a hundred years later, of the draft control effected by the use of a lamp chimney. Next came the use of kerosene, soon after the middle of the Nineteenth Century. Gas was in general use by 1850 (the city of Boston was lighted by gas in 1822) and by the close of the century came electricity.

In concluding these chapters, which are only a general introduction to the illustrations and the commentary on them, we wish to repeat that anything made in what we may speak of as a slab construction, as opposed to a frame, was built in pine, almost as a matter of course, and that anything constructed with a frame probably had the spaces between the frame filled in with pine; and possibly the frame itself was of pine, if the usage was not going to be too severe.

206

IN THE CENTRE of this photograph is what was sold at auction as a pair of old-fashioned hand-made snuffers! Actually it is one of those extremely rare rushlights that speak so vividly of primitive living. Nearly three hundred years ago those patient lips held the stalk of a burning rushlight on evenings when there was no justification for the extravagance of candles. But in any age the merest spark has been sufficient to postpone the curfew and make the proper atmosphere for sociability.

On either side is a betty lamp, one made of iron, the other of brass. Though both these lamps are of the covered type, often we find the grease container made open above, like a small saucepan.

All three of these lights are owned by Mr. F. R. Childs, Jr., of Concord, Massachusetts.

207

WOODEN SCONCES are not very often found. The problem presented something of a dilemma, for if all the draughts were shut out all the light was shut in. The inevitable compromise kept the upper portions of the room well lighted and shut out some of the air currents that swirled up from the floor. [SEE DRAWING 51.]

208

THE DESIGN of this corner light bracket is agreeably worked out.
Its height is 1 ft., 5 in. over all, the sides are 3⁄8 in. by 8 in. wide,
and the bottom 7⁄8 in. thick. The diamond glass set into the sides
measures 3 3⁄4 in. on each edge. Mrs. John C. Spring is the owner.

209

IF WE only knew the history of this lantern! There is no doubt at all about its age. The glass is thinner than 1/16 in., quite greenish, and it is utterly impossible to see anything through it, all of which characteristics are those of the diamond panes of the typical Seventeenth Century American casement window. But whether or not it is a New England or even an American piece, it is well nigh impossible to say. It was bought in Boston, and is made of pine; but pine pieces are also to be found in the Northern countries of Europe, and the tracery of the four faces is certainly not characteristic of early American work. We should expect to find geometric figures, like squares or diamonds, or arched patterns, or perhaps a heart. However that may be, the piece is really beautiful. The only means of access to the inside is through the hole on top. By pulling up the rod, a cross bar is raised and a fresh candle may be stuck in position, now at least, only by melting the base a little first. It is curious that there should be an upright runner in each corner, whereas only two of them are used. There is no evidence of there ever having been two cross bars.

The colossal compasses in the foreground were a part of some carpenter's equipment. They are pine with metal points, and belong to Mr. E. Gordon Parker, of Cambridge. [SEE DRAWING 52.]

210

HERE is an interesting corner in the Browne House at Watertown. The lantern belongs to the writer. Its frame is pine, painted red, the top piece hollowed out and domed to meet the more familiar metal cap and ring. The four short legs should be noted, as such a design at the base is less common than that of no legs. Behind the lantern is a plastered surface, the outside wall. To the right is the whitewashed partition of shadow-moulded boarding, while above are the whitewashed sticks of the framing and the single thickness of flooring of the attic.

The hinge is a splendid example of the ram's horn type, with heavy gudgeon, or upright post, from which the strap could be lifted at any time. You may see the leather washers that were used underneath the heads of the nails to take up any slack that there might be after the nails had been clinched on the other side of the doorway.

211

WE ARE open to criticism when we include a Nineteenth Century lantern in this chapter, yet the design is so simple and so entirely in keeping with those of the century preceding, that we have finally voted for it. As it was made on board a whaler, it merely bears out the writer's contention that the uniform style, that all this sort of work has, comes largely from a natural and sympathetic use of the material, unaffected by highly educated schools of taste. The bosun, fortunately, had never heard of the Greek Revival! The lantern is in the Peabody Museum at Salem.

212

THE CANDLE LANTERN is pentagonal, approximately 4 in. on a side and 9¼ in. high. The sides are made of ⅜ in. wood, each with a glass window and three holes below it for ventilation. The bottom is ⅝ in. wood with 5 holes in it for the same purpose. An iron top pierced with thirty-two 3/16 in. holes, arranged in three concentric circles, projects a veritable constellation upon the ceiling.

The stand is a ratchet light stand. The base and top are pine, but the rest is probably maple. It may be adjusted up and down, as the illustration shows.

The mirror is shown in photograph as Plate 177.

All three pieces are the property of Mr. Oliver E. Williams, of Boston and Rockport. [SEE DRAWING 50.]

213

IT IS not very often that one sees a ratchet candle stand entirely of pine. The candle in this case fits directly into the hollowed end of the ratchet. When extended, the stand measures 33 in.; when as low as it will go, as in the photograph, 27 in. The idea of the three peg feet is a sound one; three points will come to rest on any surface, no matter how uneven, while without the pegs a stand like this, on a good many of the old table and chest tops, will rock.

The lower stand is part maple and part pine, the former wood being used everywhere but in the top and the cross bar of the T. The top is 1 ft., 5½ in. square and 2 ft., 1½ in. above the floor; the post is 2 in. square.

Both pieces are in Mrs. John C. Spring's Shaker Room at West Gloucester.

CENTRE LIGHTING by chandeliers or "branches" was most appropriately used in just such a large room as this of the Brookfield Tavern, moved in modern times to Danbury, Connecticut, where for some years it was furnished with the collection of the late Mr. George F. Ives.

The middle of the three lights now belongs to Mrs. John C. Spring, of Boston. It is turned from a block of pine, which is attached to another piece of wood that suspends it at the proper height above the floor.

One should not fail to notice the decorative pile of hat boxes in the far corner, or the painted window shades.

We are endebted to *The House Beautiful* for this photograph and the one immediately following.

215

IN ANOTHER room at the Brookfield Tavern we see some more of the collection of the late Mr. George F. Ives. The chandelier that hangs over the central table is really not appropriately located, for the room is not high enough to permit lighting the candles. Yet in this low room we can see the chandelier all the better. It has a central turning, 11 in. long and 6 in. in diameter, from which the six iron arms project about 11 in. each.

216

THIS is a hanging ratchet, or to be absolutely accurate, a hanging ratchet light holder. Everything about it is made of pine, and, every part is in the original uninjured condition. The contrivance is suspended from a nail by a loop of leather. Now it would swing from a beam in the center of the room, now it would hang in the corner out of the way. On the round platform at the end would be the candle, protected from falling over and setting the house on fire by a wooden guard. Each of the two sticks measures 3 ft. in length and ½ in. by 1 in. in section. There are nineteen notches, spaced at the rate of eight to a foot. The platform or shelf, measures 4 in. by 6 in. by ¾ in. We are indebted to Mr. Franklin H. Trumbull, of New Boston, New Hampshire, for the appropriate setting.

THE TOP of the hood of this very noteworthy Seventeenth Century cradle, is missing. The panels are made of pine, but frame and turnings are hardwood, worn as rounded and as smooth as the pebbles on a beach. It has all the character of a Carver chair, and represents the same period in our history.

THERE is undeniably a great satisfaction in building something good out of such odds and ends as one happens to have on hand. The fact that three of the posts in this cradle are maple, while the fourth is oak, suggests that the builder was making the most of his limited and precious supply of sawed lumber. The turnings are beautifully patterned, those at the head being doubled at the crown. The whole cradle was held together originally by square pegs. Wormholes have appeared in both the maple of the posts and rockers and the pine boarding. [SEE DRAWING 53.]

219

THE FEELING of fellowship between this old cradle and the old house is quite striking. But why not? The frame of a house is oak, and the boards pine—and the same thing is true of the cradle. The cradle's posts are moulded and knobbed from oak 2¼ in. square. The sides are 1 in. pine boards, gouged coarsely, as a very effective means of decoration, and scalloped. Wooden pegs add considerably to the beauty, but they were put there to assist in lashing the young Puritan to his straight and narrow spot. The cradle measures 2 ft., 10½ in. long inside. It is owned by Mr. Albert H. Atkins of West Gloucester.

220

THIS CRADLE was used in the Locke family in Lexington from the year 1800 until just recently, when it was given to the Lexington Historical Society. How much older than that it is we do not know. It is a perfect example of a familiar type. The boards are all ¾ in. thick except for the covering of the hood, which is ⅜ in. Braces, fitting tightly into the angles between the rockers and the floor board, give excellent security against collapse. They are just visible in the illustration.

2 2 1

HERE is a maple and pine cradle of a very unusual design. It measures 3 ft., 2½ in. long by 1 ft., 6¾ in. wide, the posts being 2¾ in. square—which is very large. Mrs. John C. Spring has it in her house at West Gloucester.

222

HANGING CRADLES with trestle feet are later and rarer than the ordinary rocking kind. There is something about them that forecasts the age of inventions, for they hang from an ingenious contrivance that might almost have been patented! The swing, of course, follows a concave arc, whereas a rock may be described as convex. At a guess, the former is more popular with the occupant. But how are we to tell? [SEE DRAWING 54.]

223

IT IS NOT difficult to find little clothes racks, but they are not usually quite so nicely constructed. The neat mortising of the three bars into the uprights, which in turn are mortised into the trestle feet, makes a perfect piece of construction. More often the rack consists of three folding sections and therefore stands up without the need of these attractive feet. The measurements, including the tenons, are as follows: rails, ⅝ in. by 1¾ in. by 1 ft., 8¼ in.; uprights, ⅞ in. by 2 in. by 3 ft.; feet, 1½ in. by 2¼ in. by 1 ft., 1 in.

224

FOR A LONG TIME the writer had been on the lookout for a four-post bed made entirely of pine and thereby eligible for the group of miscellaneous pieces in this book. At last he found a candidate that could pass the entrance examinations. It is, perhaps, less beautiful than it is interesting. You can see, though, how the turner was thinking all the time of the fact that there must be no delicate flanges, for in pine and on anything so constantly used as a bedstead they would be sure to be broken off. That fear dominated the design, it is perfectly apparent; and it may be said to the turner's credit that the bed has come down to us in very nearly perfect condition. His error lay in choosing pine, in the first place; and possibly in living too near the middle of the nineteenth Century! The measurements are 3 ft., 7 in. by 5 ft., 8 in. inside the frame.

2 2 5

USEFUL though this box is nowadays as a waste basket, such was
not originally its duty in life. Apparently it was built to hold a
plant, for the inside of the wood is rotted badly, particularly toward the bottom. Its maker was certainly no cabinetmaker, but
he had a nice quarter-round moulding plane in his equipment.
SEE DRAWING 55.]

226

SOME CANDLES were dipped into hot tallow to be built up to their final shape; others were poured into metal moulds through which the wick had previously been threaded. Usually a set of such moulds was held in a metal rack, but occasionally the rack was made of wood, as in this instance. In a proper set all of the moulds fitted flat into the top board. This set is short several moulds and some of the vacant places have been filled with individual tubes whose handles keep them from settling into place. The rack is 1 ft., 8 in. long, 7½ in. wide and 1 ft., 2 in. high. The wood is ⅞ in. on the sides and ⅝ on the top and bottom.

227

CHECKERS AND CHESS, as games are no infants like bridge and crossword puzzles. This particular board is constructed of a centrepiece ¾ in. thick and 1 ft., 4 in. square, bordered by a little fence ⅜ in. by 1⅛ in. nailed flush on the bottom. The checker pattern is painted in 1⅛ in. squares of black and red on a dark green background. Mr. E. Gordon Parker owns the wooden bowles and the mortar and pestle, and the writer owns the checkerboard.

228

THIS LITTLE PINE HORSE has a curiously *art nouveau* appearance. He is just an impression, without too much regard for anatomical perfection. He is cut out of a block of pine ten inches high, ten inches wide, and two and a quarter inches thick. The painting is still in good condition; black mane and hoofs (the tail is missing) and a dark bay body. The property of Mr. Samuel Temple, of Lynnfield, Massachusetts.

229

YOU CAN SAY all sorts of things about this fellow, but you must admit he is unique, and very decorative. Do not miss the birds among the leaves. Mr. Samuel Temple, of Lynnfield, who grants permission to give the reindeer all this publicity, says he was purchased in Massachusetts. However, as he has so much European feeling, we are putting him in as a tailpiece, so that those who would otherwise point back with much concern to the *Early New England* part of the title may close the book a page before the others.

DRAWINGS

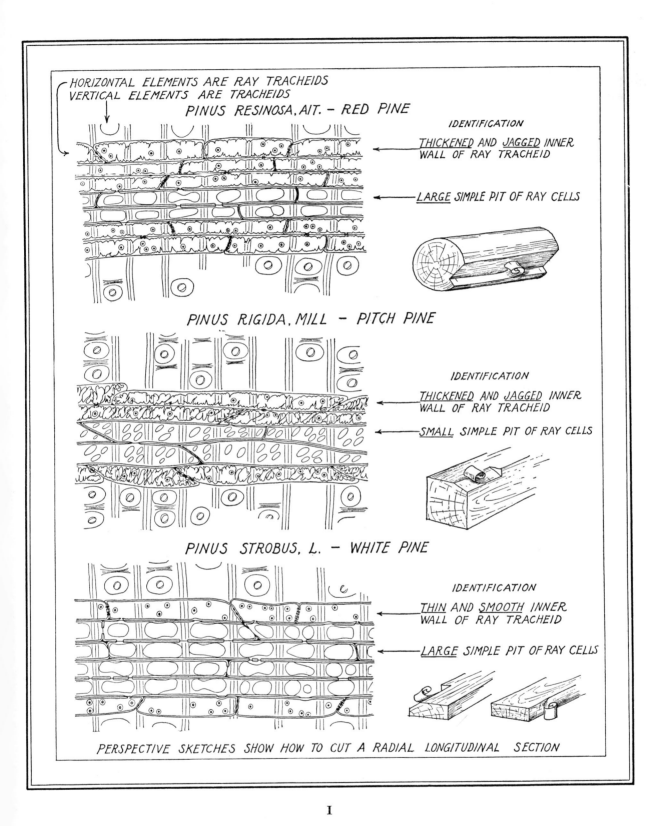

HORIZONTAL ELEMENTS ARE RAY TRACHEIDS
VERTICAL ELEMENTS ARE TRACHEIDS

PINUS RESINOSA, AIT. - RED PINE

IDENTIFICATION

THICKENED AND JAGGED INNER
WALL OF RAY TRACHEID

LARGE SIMPLE PIT OF RAY CELLS

PINUS RIGIDA, MILL - PITCH PINE

IDENTIFICATION

THICKENED AND JAGGED INNER
WALL OF RAY TRACHEID

SMALL SIMPLE PIT OF RAY CELLS

PINUS STROBUS, L. - WHITE PINE

IDENTIFICATION

THIN AND SMOOTH INNER
WALL OF RAY TRACHEID

LARGE SIMPLE PIT OF RAY CELLS

PERSPECTIVE SKETCHES SHOW HOW TO CUT A RADIAL LONGITUDINAL SECTION

I

Microscopic Radial Longitudinal Sections of Pine Wood

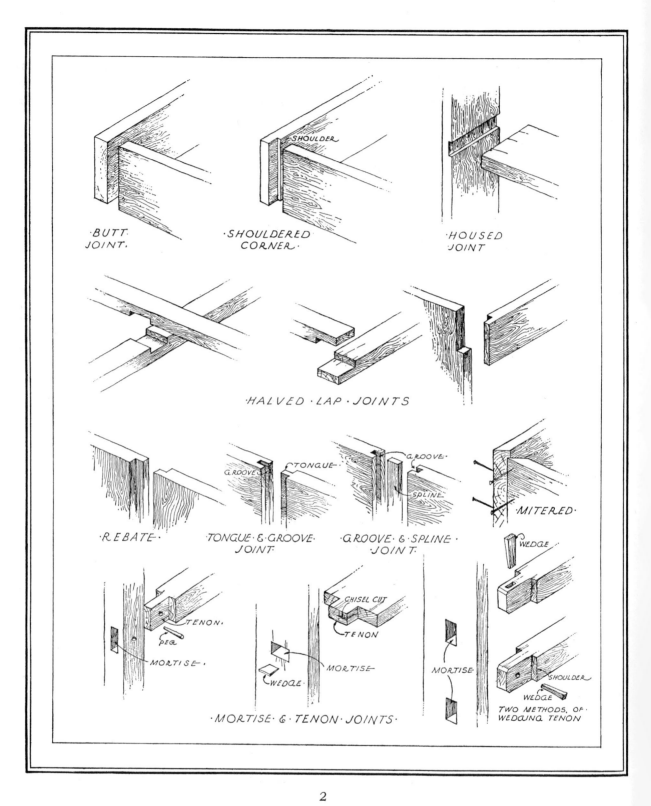

·BUTT· JOINT·

·SHOULDERED CORNER·

·HOUSED JOINT·

·HALVED·LAP·JOINTS·

·REBATE·

TONGUE·&·GROOVE· JOINT·

·GROOVE·&·SPLINE· JOINT·

·MITERED·

·MORTISE·&·TENON·JOINTS·

TWO METHODS OF WEDGING TENON

2

Types of Jointing

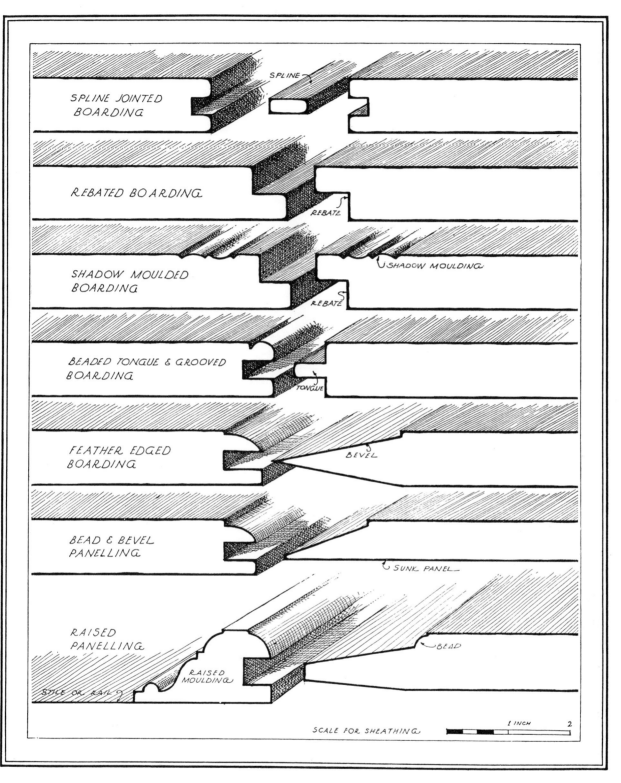

SPLINE JOINTED
BOARDING

SPLINE

REBATED BOARDING

REBATE

SHADOW MOULDED
BOARDING

SHADOW MOULDING

REBATE

BEADED TONGUE & GROOVED
BOARDING

TONGUE

FEATHER EDGED
BOARDING

BEVEL

BEAD & BEVEL
PANELLING

SUNK PANEL

RAISED
PANELLING

RAISED
MOULDING

STILE OR RAIL

BEAD

SCALE FOR SHEATHING

1 INCH   2

3

Types of Sheathing and Panelling

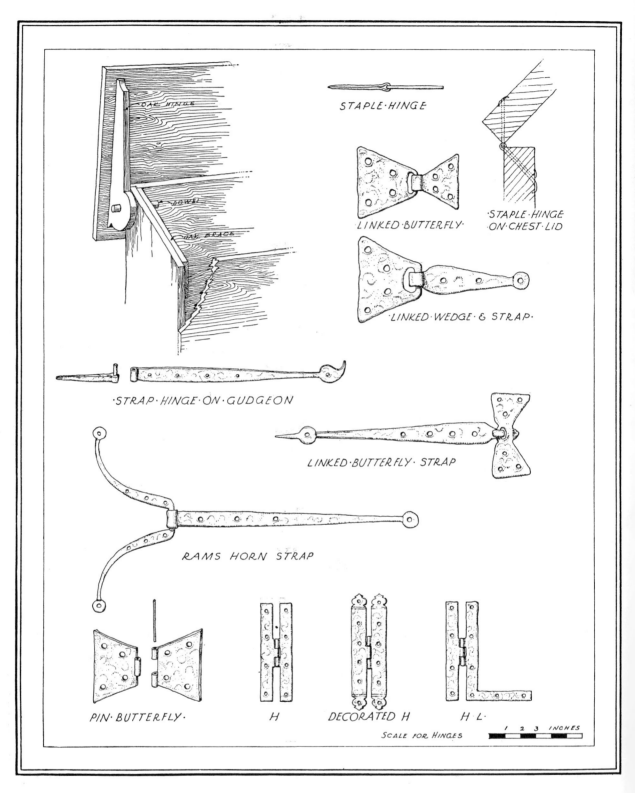

OAK HINGE

DOWEL

OAK BRACE

STAPLE·HINGE

LINKED·BUTTERFLY

·STAPLE·HINGE
ON·CHEST·LID

·LINKED·WEDGE·&·STRAP.

·STRAP·HINGE·ON·GUDGEON·

LINKED·BUTTERFLY·STRAP

RAMS HORN STRAP

PIN·BUTTERFLY·

H

DECORATED H

H L

SCALE FOR HINGES

1   2   3   INCHES

4

The Development of Hinges

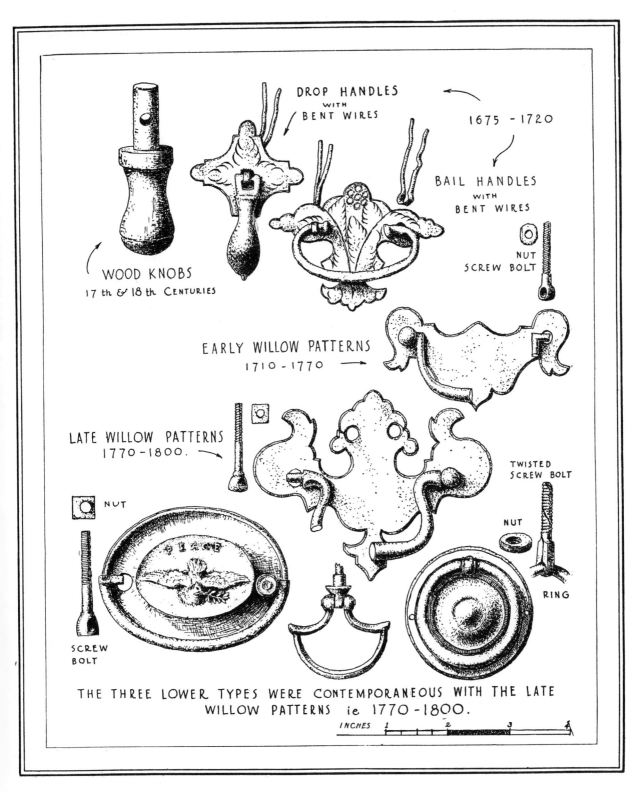

DROP HANDLES
WITH
BENT WIRES

1675 - 1720

BAIL HANDLES
WITH
BENT WIRES

NUT
SCREW BOLT

WOOD KNOBS
17 th & 18 th Centuries

EARLY WILLOW PATTERNS
1710 - 1770

LATE WILLOW PATTERNS
1770 - 1800.

TWISTED
SCREW BOLT

NUT

NUT

RING

SCREW
BOLT

THE THREE LOWER TYPES WERE CONTEMPORANEOUS WITH THE LATE
WILLOW PATTERNS ie 1770 - 1800.

INCHES 1 2 3 4

5

The Development of Drawer Pulls

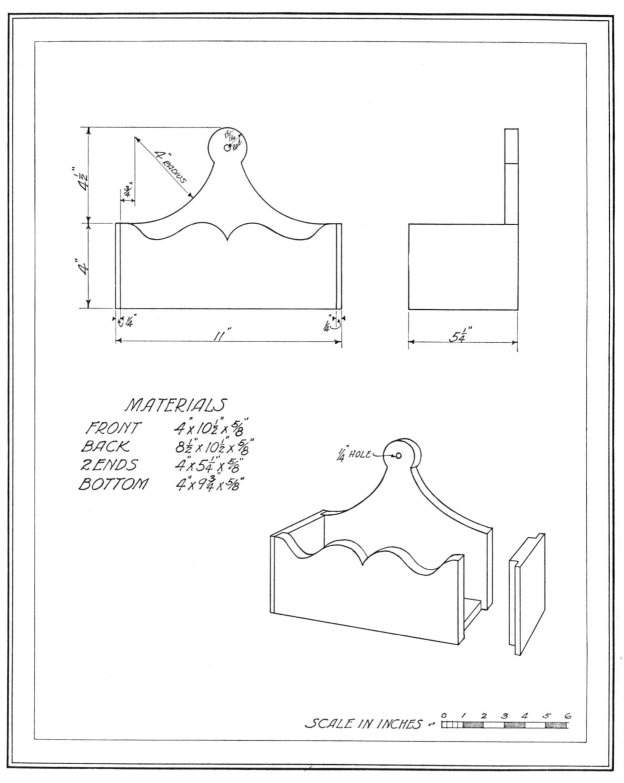

MATERIALS

FRONT $4'' \times 10\frac{1}{2}'' \times \frac{5}{8}''$
BACK $8\frac{1}{2}'' \times 10\frac{1}{2}'' \times \frac{5}{8}''$
2 ENDS $4'' \times 5\frac{1}{4}'' \times \frac{5}{8}''$
BOTTOM $4'' \times 9\frac{3}{4}'' \times \frac{5}{8}''$

SCALE IN INCHES

Open Wall Box [SEE PLATE I]

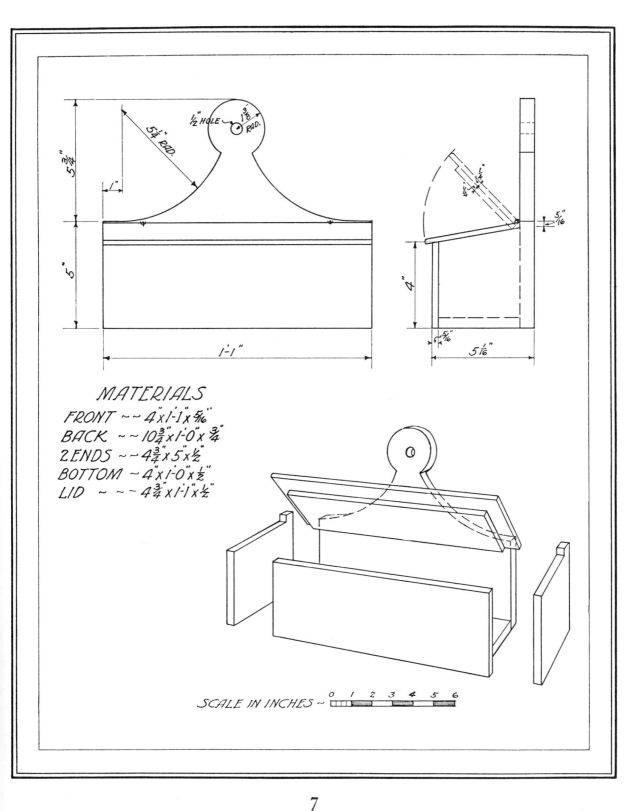

MATERIALS
FRONT ~~ 4"x1-1"x 5/16"
BACK ~~ 10¾"x1'-0"x ¾"
2 ENDS ~~ 4¾"x5"x½"
BOTTOM ~ 4"x1'-0"x½"
LID ~ ~ 4¾"x1-1"x½"

SCALE IN INCHES ~ 0 1 2 3 4 5 6

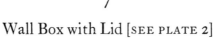

7

Wall Box with Lid [SEE PLATE 2]

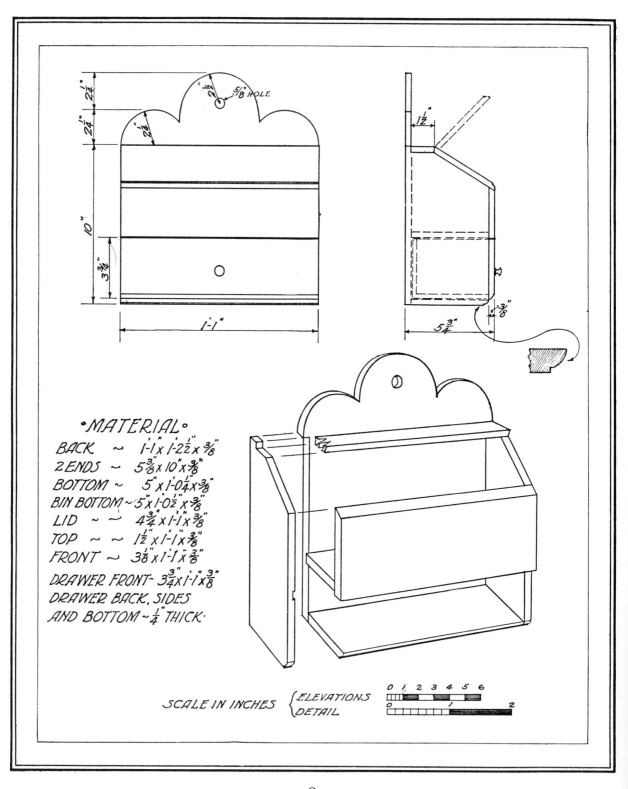

•MATERIAL•

BACK ~ 1'-1" x 1'-2½" x ⅜"
2 ENDS ~ 5⅜" x 10" x ⅜"
BOTTOM ~ 5" x 1'-0¼" x ⅜"
BIN BOTTOM ~ 5" x 1'-0½" x ⅜"
LID ~ ~ 4¾" x 1'-1" x ⅜"
TOP ~ ~ 1½" x 1'-1" x ⅜"
FRONT ~ 3⅛" x 1'-1" x ⅜"
DRAWER FRONT~ 3¾" x 1'-1" x ⅜"
DRAWER BACK, SIDES
AND BOTTOM ~ ¼" THICK·

SCALE IN INCHES { ELEVATIONS
                 { DETAIL

8

Wall Box with One Drawer [SEE PLATE 3]

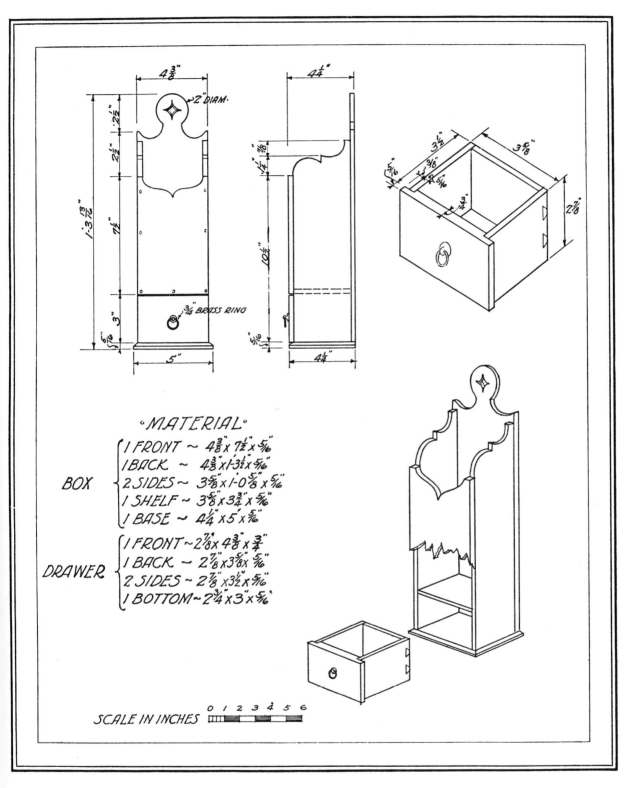

·MATERIAL·

BOX
- 1 FRONT ~ $4\frac{3}{8}$" x $7\frac{1}{2}$" x $\frac{5}{16}$"
- 1 BACK ~ $4\frac{3}{8}$" x 1'-$3\frac{1}{2}$" x $\frac{5}{16}$"
- 2 SIDES ~ $3\frac{5}{8}$" x 1'-0$\frac{5}{8}$" x $\frac{5}{16}$"
- 1 SHELF ~ $3\frac{5}{8}$" x $3\frac{3}{4}$" x $\frac{5}{16}$"
- 1 BASE ~ $4\frac{1}{4}$" x 5" x $\frac{5}{16}$"

DRAWER
- 1 FRONT ~ $2\frac{7}{8}$" x $4\frac{3}{8}$" x $\frac{3}{4}$"
- 1 BACK ~ $2\frac{7}{8}$" x $3\frac{5}{8}$" x $\frac{5}{16}$"
- 2 SIDES ~ $2\frac{7}{8}$" x $3\frac{1}{2}$" x $\frac{5}{16}$"
- 1 BOTTOM ~ $2\frac{3}{4}$" x 3" x $\frac{5}{16}$"

SCALE IN INCHES   0 1 2 3 4 5 6

9

Long Pipe Box with One Drawer [SEE PLATE 6]

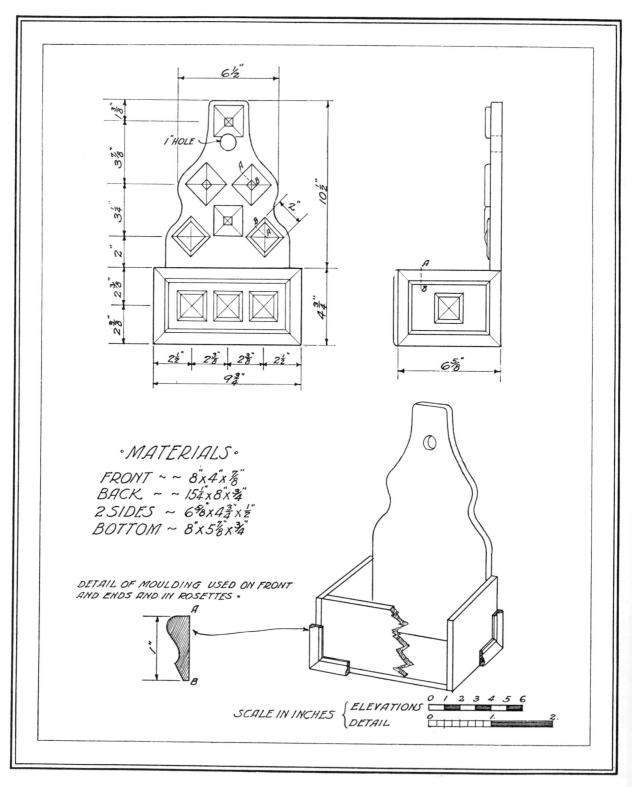

$6\frac{1}{2}''$

$1\frac{3}{8}''$

$3\frac{7}{8}''$

1" HOLE

$10\frac{1}{2}''$

A

B

2"

$3\frac{1}{4}''$

B

A

2"

$2\frac{3}{8}''$

$4\frac{3}{4}''$

$2\frac{3}{8}''$

A

B

$2\frac{1}{2}''$ $2\frac{3}{8}''$ $2\frac{3}{8}''$ $2\frac{1}{2}''$

$9\frac{3}{4}''$

$6\frac{5}{8}''$

·MATERIALS·

FRONT ~ ~ 8"x4"x⅞"
BACK ~ ~ 15¼"x8"x¾"
2 SIDES ~ 6⅝"x4¾"x½"
BOTTOM ~ 8"x5⅞"x¾"

DETAIL OF MOULDING USED ON FRONT
AND ENDS AND IN ROSETTES·

A

1"

B

SCALE IN INCHES { ELEVATIONS
{ DETAIL

0 1 2 3 4 5 6

0 1 2

10

Decorated Pipe Box [SEE PLATE 10]

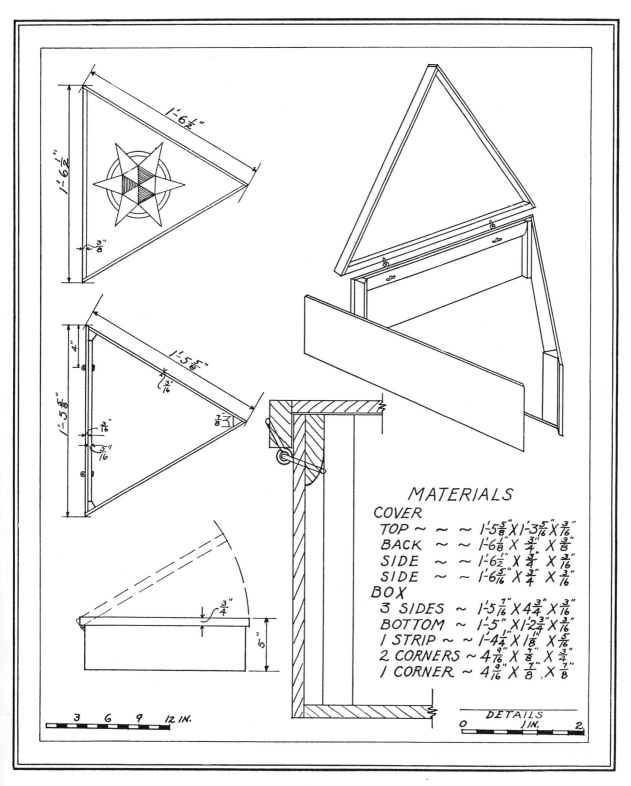

MATERIALS

COVER
TOP ~ ~ ~ $1'$-$5\frac{5}{8}''$ X $1'$-$3\frac{5}{16}''$ X $\frac{3}{16}''$
BACK ~ ~ $1'$-$6\frac{1}{8}''$ X $\frac{3}{4}''$ X $\frac{3}{8}''$
SIDE ~ ~ $1'$-$6\frac{1}{2}''$ X $\frac{3}{4}''$ X $\frac{3}{16}''$
SIDE ~ ~ $1'$-$6\frac{5}{16}''$ X $\frac{3}{4}''$ X $\frac{3}{16}''$
BOX
3 SIDES ~ $1'$-$5\frac{1}{16}''$ X $4\frac{3}{4}''$ X $\frac{3}{16}''$
BOTTOM ~ $1'$-$5''$ X $1'$-$2\frac{3}{4}''$ X $\frac{3}{16}''$
1 STRIP ~ ~ $1'$-$4\frac{1}{4}''$ X $1\frac{1}{8}''$ X $\frac{5}{16}''$
2 CORNERS ~ $4\frac{9}{16}''$ X $\frac{7}{8}''$ X $\frac{3}{4}''$
1 CORNER ~ $4\frac{9}{16}''$ X $\frac{7}{8}''$ X $\frac{7}{8}''$

DETAILS
0 ___ 1 IN. ___ 2.

3   6   9   12 IN.

11

Cocked Hat Box [SEE PLATE 19]

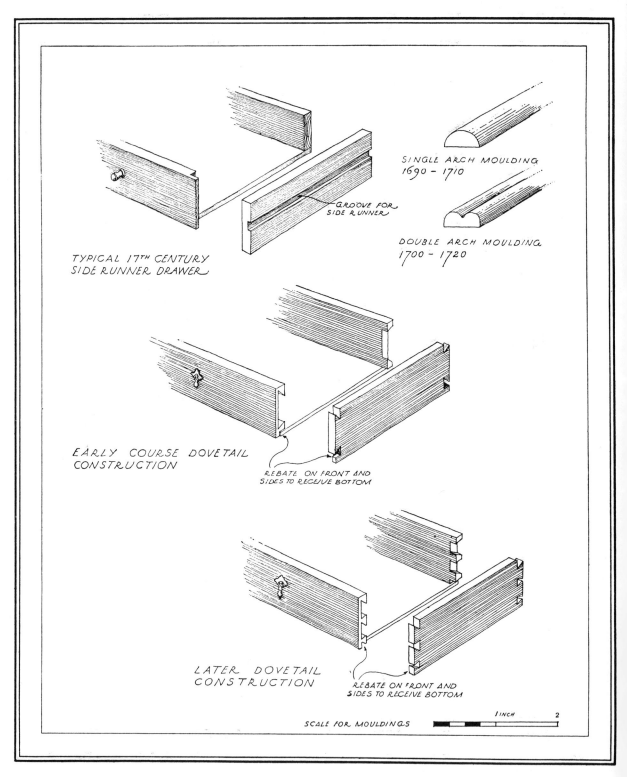

SINGLE ARCH MOULDING
1690 – 1710

DOUBLE ARCH MOULDING
1700 – 1720

GROOVE FOR
SIDE RUNNER

TYPICAL 17TH CENTURY
SIDE RUNNER DRAWER

EARLY COURSE DOVETAIL
CONSTRUCTION

REBATE ON FRONT AND
SIDES TO RECEIVE BOTTOM

LATER DOVETAIL
CONSTRUCTION

REBATE ON FRONT AND
SIDES TO RECEIVE BOTTOM

SCALE FOR MOULDINGS

1 INCH   2

I 2

The Development of Drawer Construction

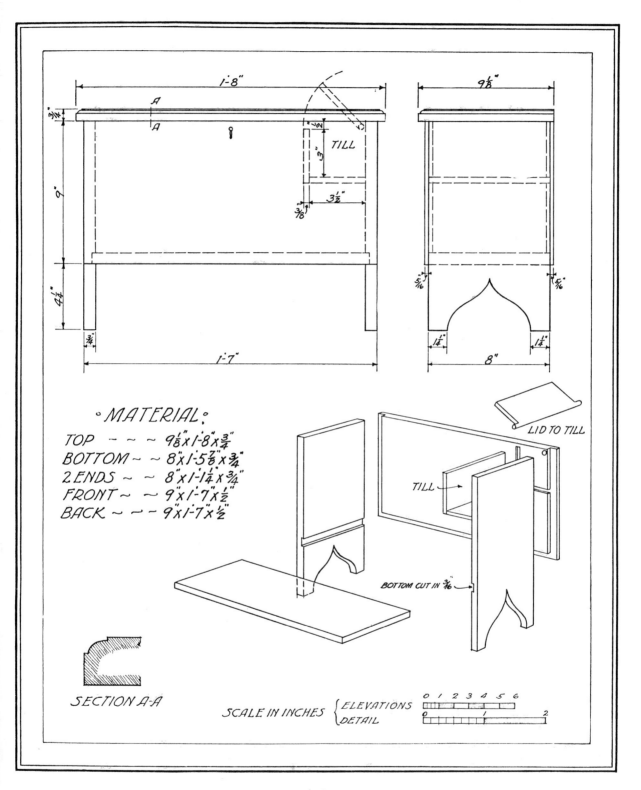

TILL

·MATERIAL·

TOP ~ ~ ~ 9⅛"x1-8"x¾"
BOTTOM ~ ~ 8"x1-5⅞"x¾"
2 ENDS ~ ~ 8"x1-1¼"x¾"
FRONT ~ ~ 9"x1-7"x½"
BACK ~ ~ ~ 9"x1-7"x½"

LID TO TILL

TILL

BOTTOM CUT IN ³⁄₁₆

SECTION A-A

SCALE IN INCHES { ELEVATIONS | DETAIL }

0 1 2 3 4 5 6

0 1 2

1 3

Small Six-Board Chest [SEE PLATE 30]

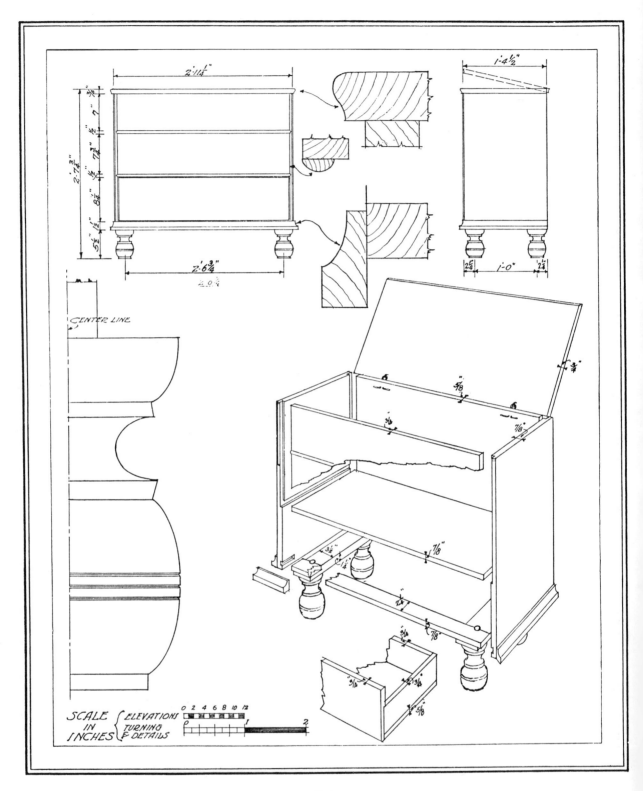

Ball-Foot Blanket Chest [SEE PLATE 35]

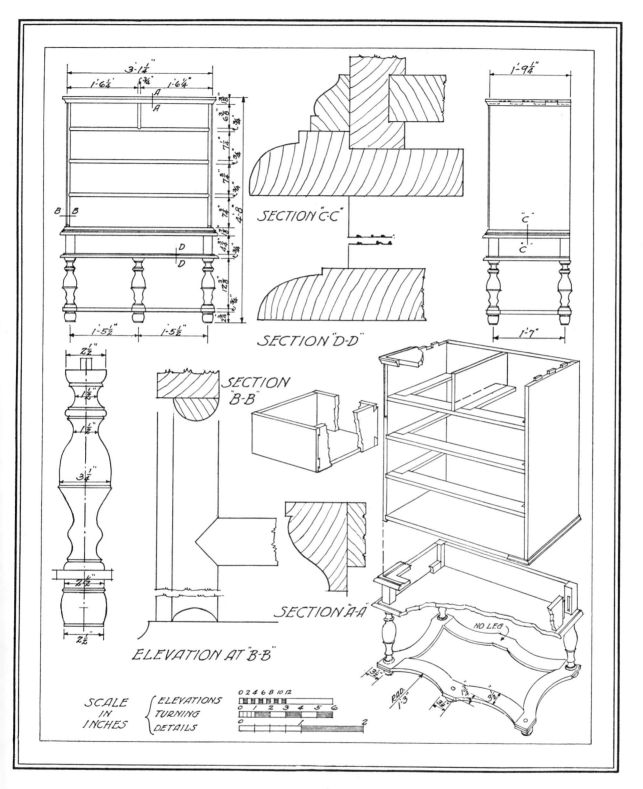

SECTION "C-C"

SECTION "D-D"

SECTION "B-B"

SECTION "A-A"

ELEVATION AT "B-B"

NO LEG

RAD. 1'-3"

SCALE
IN
INCHES

ELEVATIONS
TURNING
DETAILS

0 2 4 6 8 10 12

0 1 2 3 4 5 6

0 1 2

15

Chest on Frame with Painted Decoration [SEE PLATE 45]

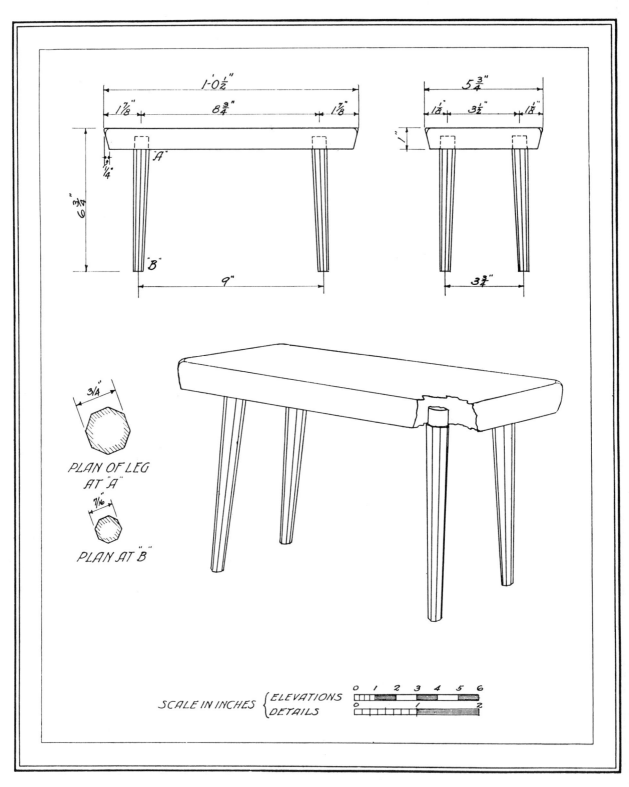

1'-0½"

1⅞" 8¾" 1⅞"

5¾"

1⅛" 3½" 1⅛"

1"

"A"

¾¼"

6¾"

"B"

9"

3¾"

¾"

PLAN OF LEG
AT "A"

7/16"

PLAN AT "B"

SCALE IN INCHES {ELEVATIONS
                 {DETAILS

0 1 2 3 4 5 6

0   1   2

16

Simple Footstool with Octagonal Legs [SEE PLATE 51]

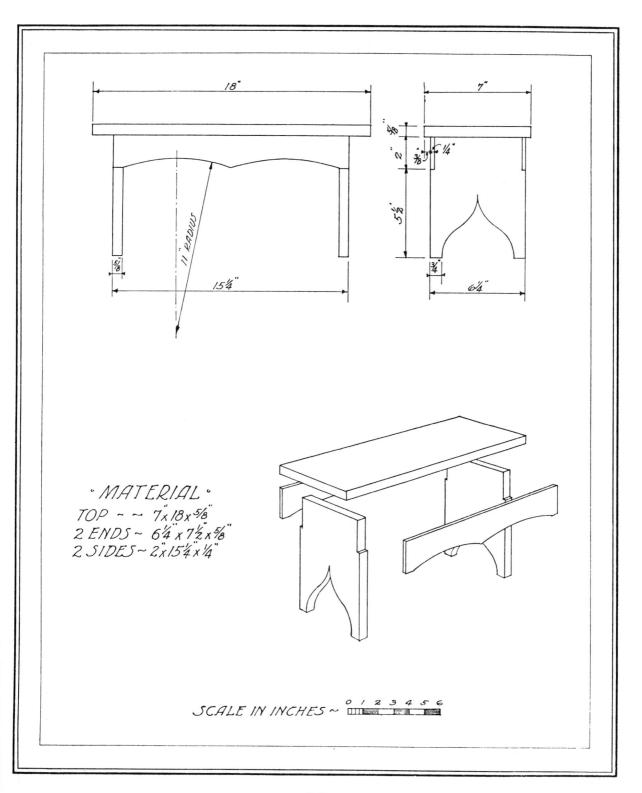

· MATERIAL ·
TOP ~ ~ 7"x 18 x 5/8"
2 ENDS ~ 6¼" x 7½" x 5/8"
2 SIDES ~ 2"x 15¼" x ¼"

SCALE IN INCHES ~ 0 1 2 3 4 5 6

I 7

Five-Board Footstool [SEE PLATE 53]

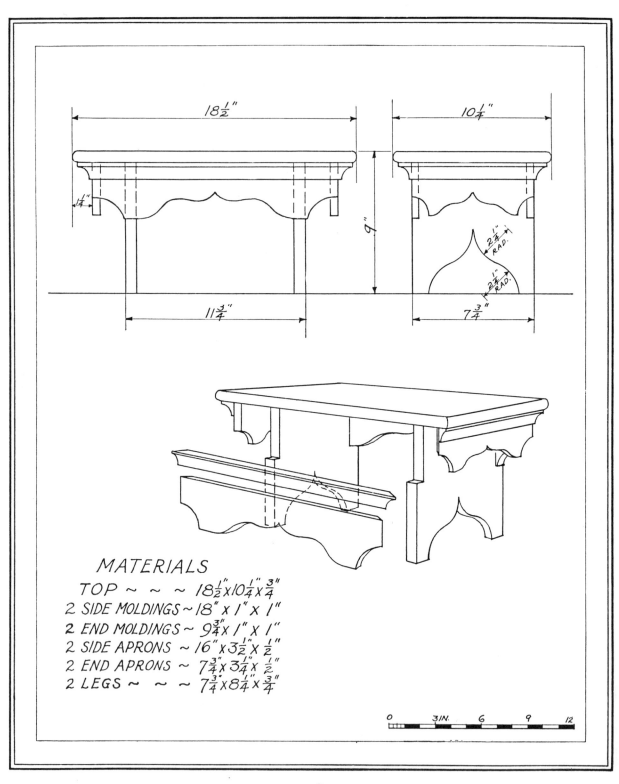

18½" 10¼"

9"

11¾" 7¾"

2¼" RAD.

2¼" RAD.

1¼"

MATERIALS
TOP ~ ~ ~ 18½" x 10¼" x ¾"
2 SIDE MOLDINGS ~ 18" x 1" x 1"
2 END MOLDINGS ~ 9¾" x 1" x 1"
2 SIDE APRONS ~ 16" x 3½" x ½"
2 END APRONS ~ 7¾" x 3¼" x ½"
2 LEGS ~ ~ ~ 7¾" x 8¼" x ¾"

0   3 IN.   6   9   12

Footstool with Four Aprons [SEE PLATE 57]

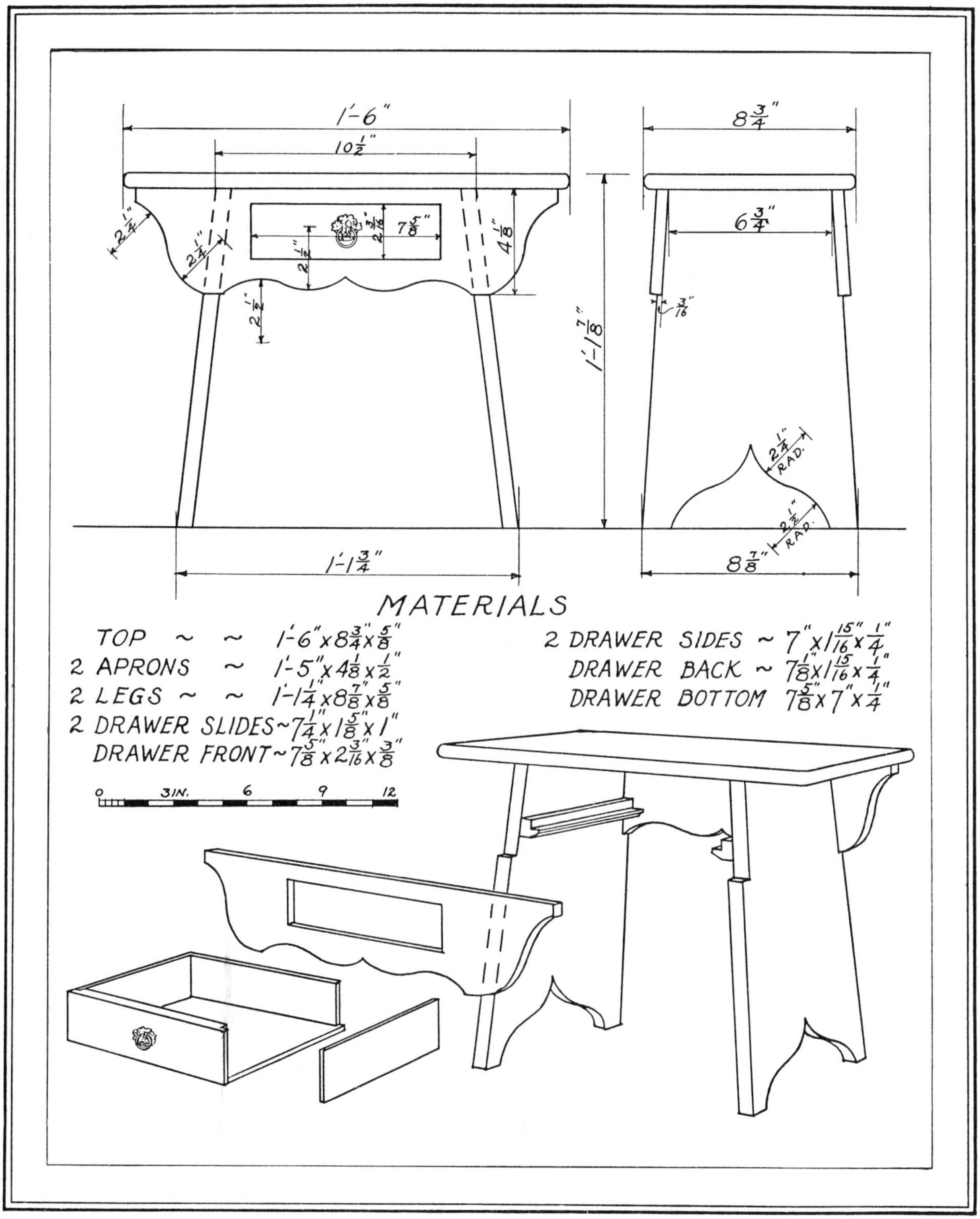
1'-6"
10 1/2"
8 3/4"
6 3/4"
1'-1 7/8"
1'-1 3/4"
8 7/8"
2 1/4" RAD.
2 1/2" RAD.
MATERIALS
TOP ~ ~ 1'-6" x 8 3/4" x 5/8"
2 APRONS ~ 1'-5" x 4 1/8" x 1/2"
2 LEGS ~ ~ 1'-1 1/4" x 8 7/8" x 5/8"
2 DRAWER SLIDES ~ 7 1/4" x 1 5/8" x 1"
DRAWER FRONT ~ 7 5/8" x 2 3/16" x 3/8"
2 DRAWER SIDES ~ 7" x 1 15/16" x 1/4"
DRAWER BACK ~ 7 1/8" x 1 15/16" x 1/4"
DRAWER BOTTOM 7 5/8" x 7" x 1/4"
0 3 IN. 6 9 12

19

Footstool with Drawer [SEE PLATE 58]

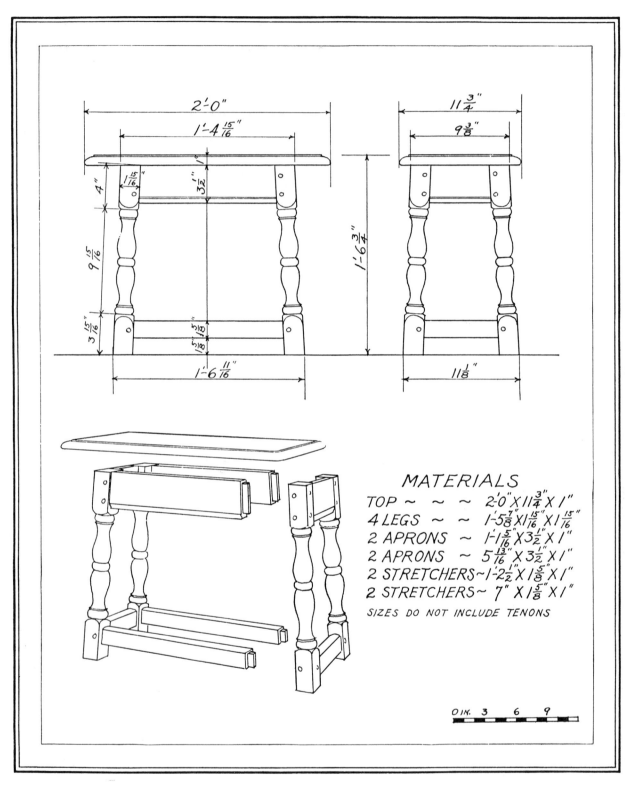

MATERIALS

TOP ~ ~ ~ 2'-0" X 11¾" X 1"
4 LEGS ~ ~ 1'-5⅞" X 1¹⁵⁄₁₆" X 1¹⁵⁄₁₆"
2 APRONS ~ 1'-1⁵⁄₁₆" X 3½" X 1"
2 APRONS ~ 5¹³⁄₁₆" X 3½" X 1"
2 STRETCHERS ~ 1'-2½" X 1⅝" X 1"
2 STRETCHERS ~ 7" X 1⅝" X 1"

SIZES DO NOT INCLUDE TENONS

0 IN.   3   6   9

20

Joined Stool [SEE PLATE 60]

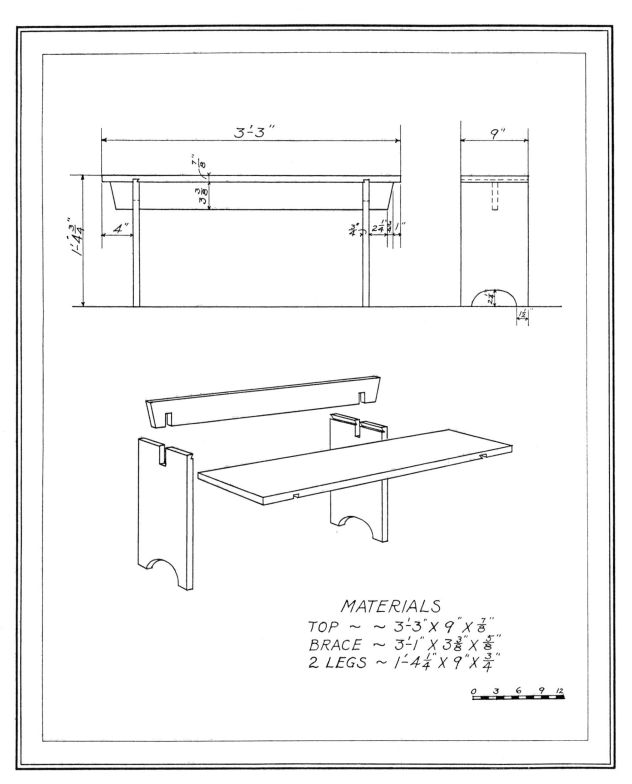

MATERIALS
TOP ~ ~ 3'-3" X 9" X $\frac{7}{8}$"
BRACE ~ 3'-1" X 3$\frac{3}{8}$" X $\frac{5}{8}$"
2 LEGS ~ 1'-4$\frac{1}{4}$" X 9" X $\frac{3}{4}$"

21

Centre-Braced Form [SEE PLATE 63]

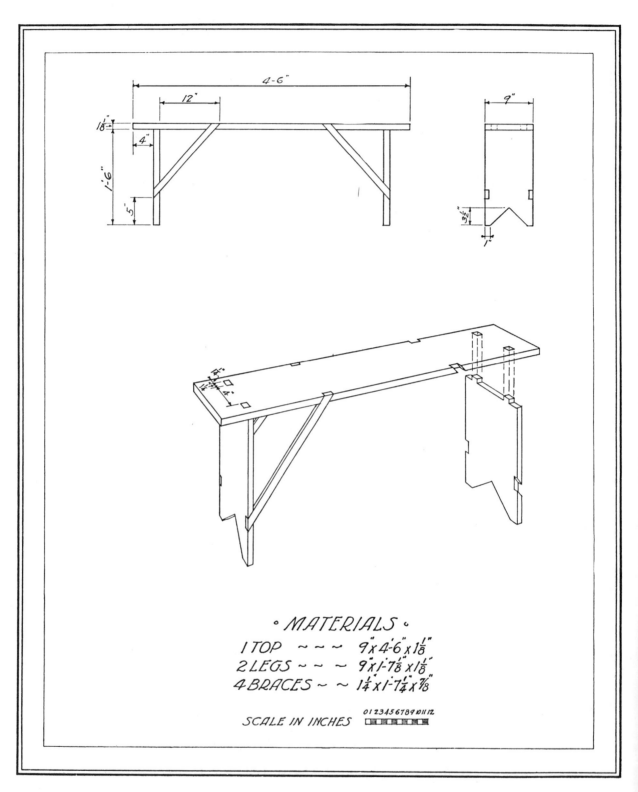

° MATERIALS °
1 TOP ~ ~ ~ 9"x 4'-6"x 1⅛"
2 LEGS ~ ~ ~ 9"x 1'-7⅞"x 1⅛"
4 BRACES ~ ~ 1¼"x 1'-7¼"x ⅞"

SCALE IN INCHES
0 1 2 3 4 5 6 7 8 9 10 11 12

22

Form with Slanting Braces [SEE PLATE 64]

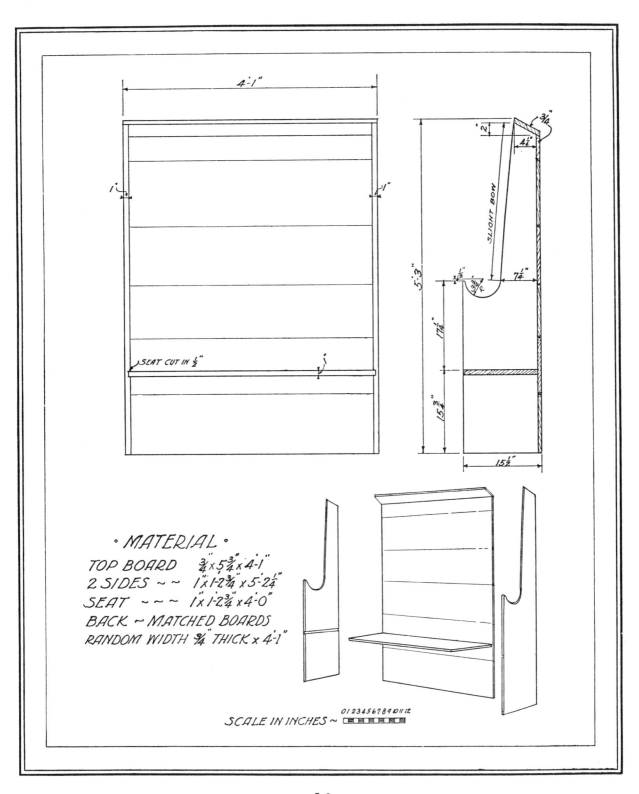

· MATERIAL ·

TOP BOARD $\frac{3}{4}'' \times 5\frac{3}{4}'' \times 4'-1''$
2 SIDES ~ ~ $1'' \times 1'-2\frac{3}{4}'' \times 5'-2\frac{1}{4}''$
SEAT ~ ~ ~ $1'' \times 1'-2\frac{3}{4}'' \times 4'-0''$
BACK ~ MATCHED BOARDS
RANDOM WIDTH $\frac{3}{4}''$ THICK × $4'-1''$

SCALE IN INCHES ~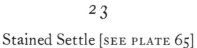

23

Stained Settle [SEE PLATE 65]

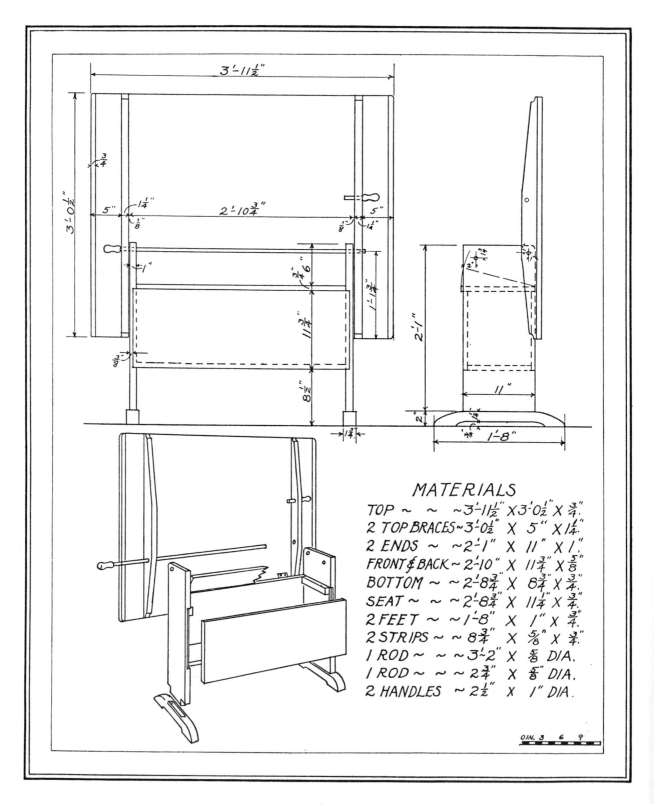

MATERIALS

TOP ~ ~ ~3'-11½" X 3'-0½" X ¾".
2 TOP BRACES ~ 3'-0½" X 5" X 1¼".
2 ENDS ~ ~2'-1" X 11" X 1".
FRONT & BACK ~ 2'-10" X 11¾" X ⅝".
BOTTOM ~ ~2'-8¾" X 8¾" X ¾".
SEAT ~ ~ ~2'-8¾" X 11¼" X ¾".
2 FEET ~ ~1'-8" X 1" X ¾".
2 STRIPS ~ ~ 8¾" X ⅝" X ¾".
1 ROD ~ ~ ~3'-2" X ⅝" DIA.
1 ROD ~ ~ ~2¾" X ⅝" DIA.
2 HANDLES ~ 2½" X 1" DIA.

OIN. 3   6   9

24

Settle Table [SEE PLATE 70]

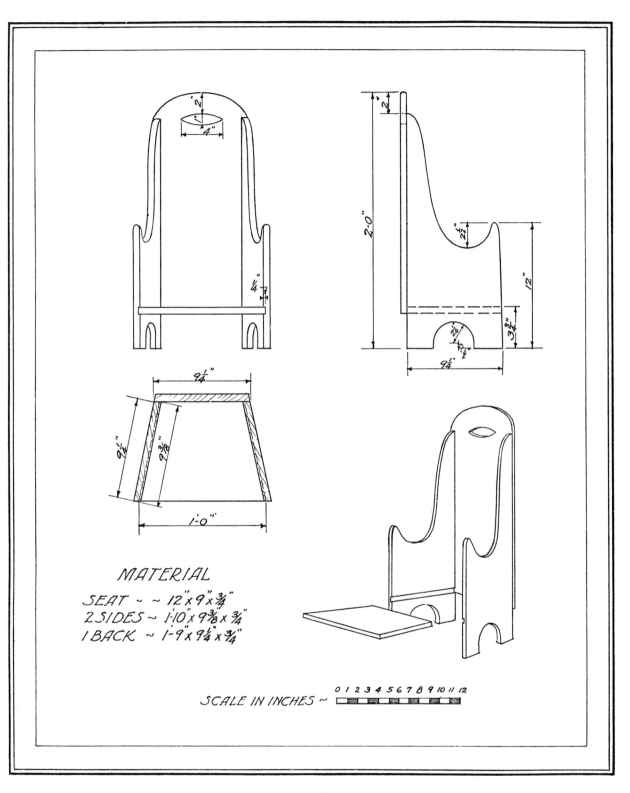

MATERIAL

SEAT ~ ~ 12"x9"x¾"
2 SIDES ~ 1'-10"x9⅜"x¾"
1 BACK ~ 1'-9"x9¼"x¾"

SCALE IN INCHES ~ 0 1 2 3 4 5 6 7 8 9 10 11 12

25

Child's Chair [SEE PLATE 74]

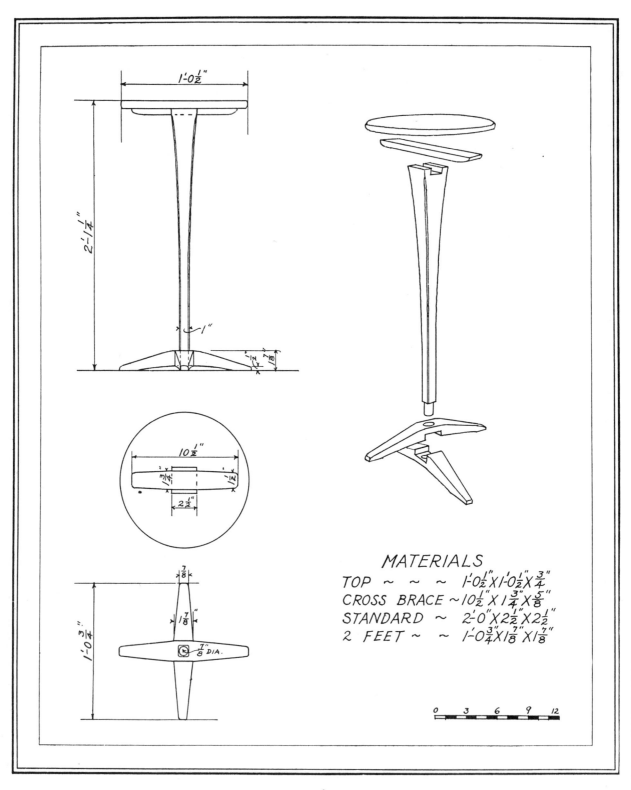

MATERIALS
TOP ~ ~ ~ 1'-0½"×1'-0½"×¾"
CROSS BRACE ~10½"×1¾"×⅝"
STANDARD ~ 2'-0"×2½"×2½"
2 FEET ~ ~ 1'-0¾"×1⅞"×1⅞"

26

Candle Stand with Claw Foot [SEE PLATE 77]

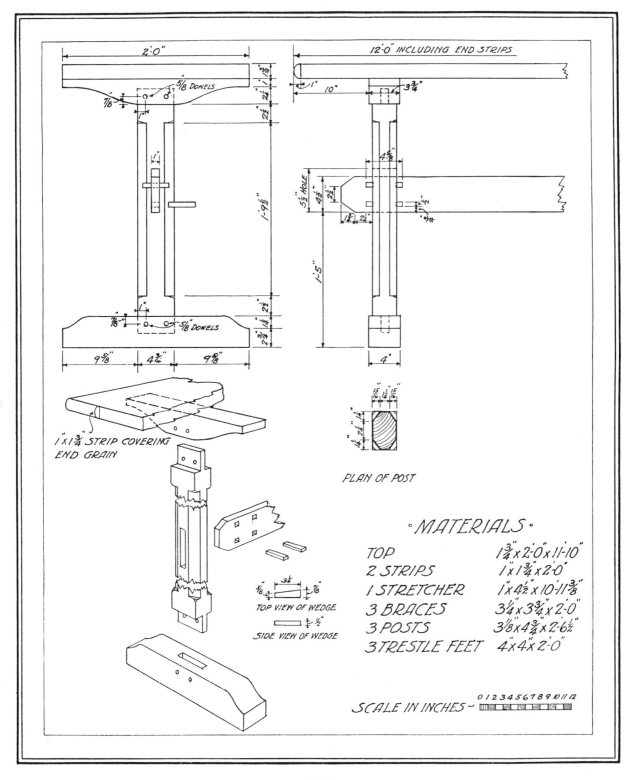

2'-0"

5/8 Dowels

7/8"

1'-9½"

5/8 DOWELS

7/8"

9⅝"   4¾"   9⅝"

12'-0" INCLUDING END STRIPS

1"   10"   3¾"

4⅝"

5½" HOLE   4½"   2¼"

1'-5"

1¾" 2¼"

4"

PLAN OF POST

1"×1¾" STRIP COVERING
END GRAIN

TOP VIEW OF WEDGE

SIDE VIEW OF WEDGE

· MATERIALS ·

TOP	1¾" × 2'-0" × 11'-10"
2 STRIPS	1" × 1¾" × 2'-0"
1 STRETCHER	1" × 4½" × 10'-11⅜"
3 BRACES	¾" × 3¾" × 2'-0"
3 POSTS	3⅛" × 4¾" × 2'-6½"
3 TRESTLE FEET	4" × 4" × 2'-0"

0 1 2 3 4 5 6 7 8 9 10 11 12

SCALE IN INCHES ~

27

The Grand Trestle Table [SEE PLATE 82]

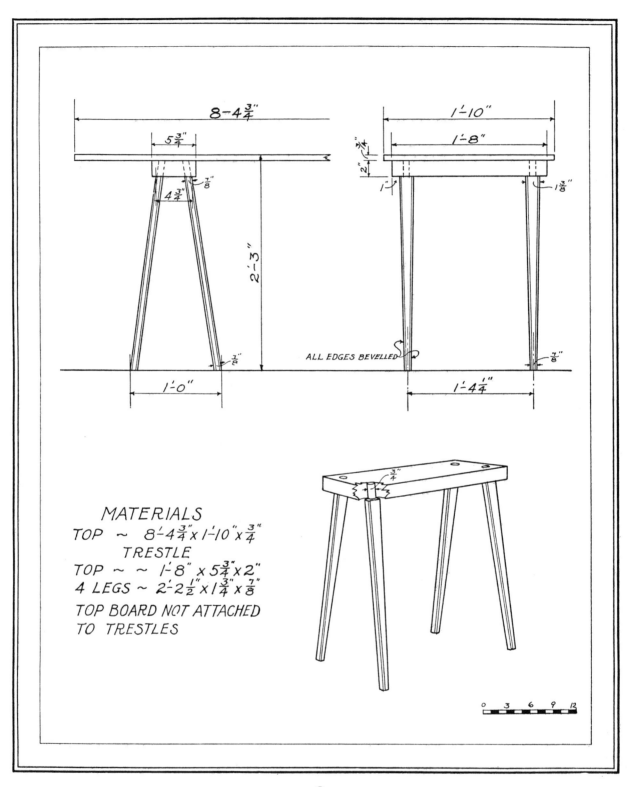

MATERIALS
TOP ~ 8′-4¾″ x 1′-10″ x ¾″
    TRESTLE
TOP ~ ~ 1′-8″ x 5¾″ x 2″
4 LEGS ~ 2′-2½″ x 1¾″ x ⅞″

TOP BOARD NOT ATTACHED
TO TRESTLES

ALL EDGES BEVELLED

0 3 6 9 12

28

Lighter Trestle Table [SEE PLATE 83]

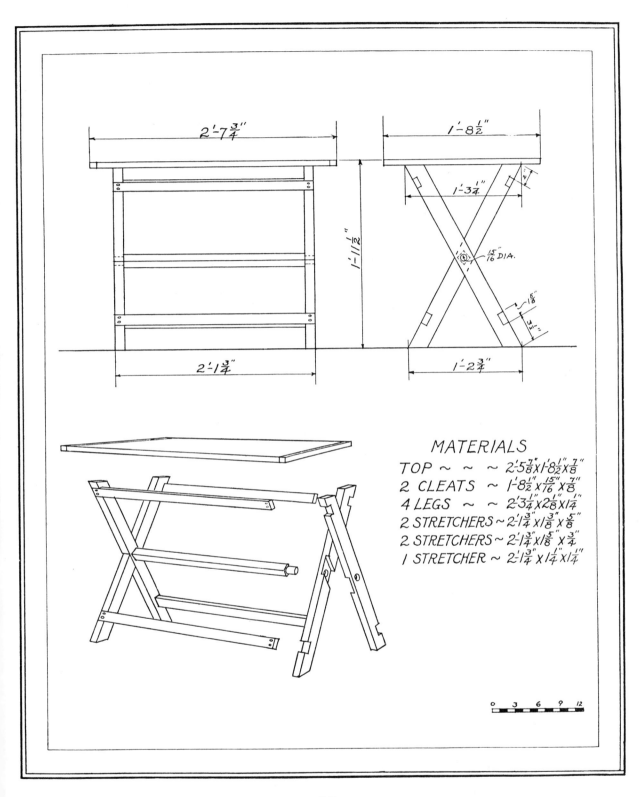

MATERIALS

TOP ~ ~ ~ 2'-5⅞"x1'-8½"x⅞"
2 CLEATS ~ 1'-8½"x15/16"x⅞"
4 LEGS ~ ~ 2'-3¼"x2⅛"x1¼"
2 STRETCHERS ~ 2'-1¾"x1⅜"x⅝"
2 STRETCHERS~ 2'-1¾"x1⅝"x¾"
1 STRETCHER ~ 2'-1¾"x1¼"x1¼"

29

"X"-Trestle Table [SEE PLATE 84]

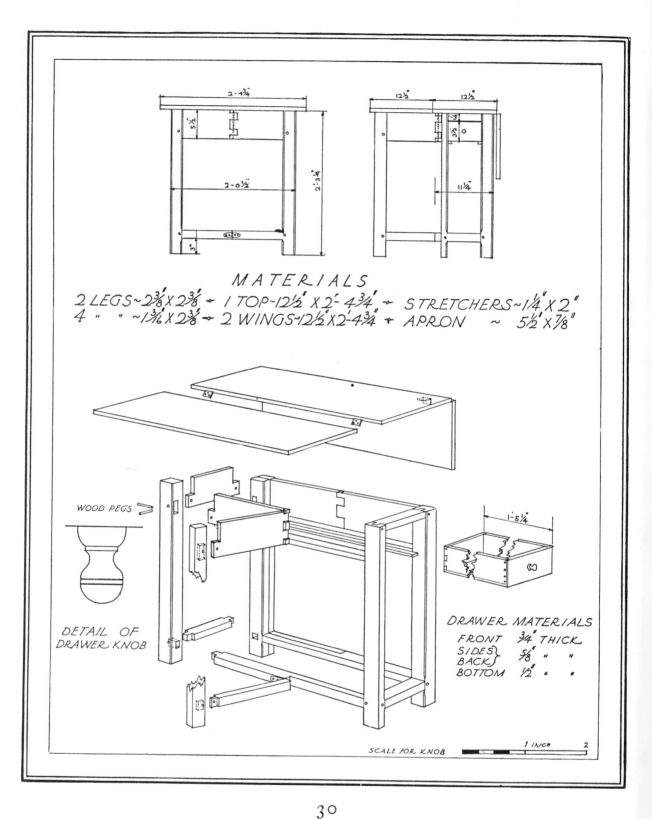

MATERIALS

2 LEGS ~ 2⅜" X 2⅜" ~ 1 TOP ~ 12½" X 2'- 4¾" ~ STRETCHERS ~ 1¼" X 2"

4 " " ~ 1³/₁₆" X 2⅜" ~ 2 WINGS ~ 12½" X 2'-4¾" ~ APRON ~ 5½" X ⅞"

WOOD PEGS

DETAIL OF
DRAWER KNOB

1'-5¼"

3

DRAWER MATERIALS

FRONT   ¾" THICK
SIDES } ⅝" "   "
BACK }
BOTTOM ½" "   "

SCALE FOR KNOB   1 INCH   2

30

Split Gate-Leg Table [SEE PLATE 87]

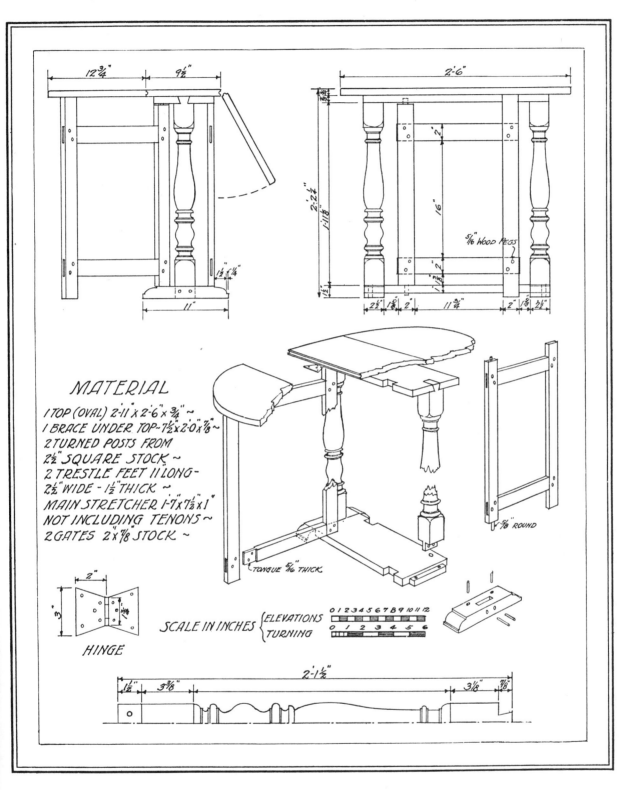

MATERIAL

1 TOP (OVAL) 2'-11" x 2'-6" x 3/4" ~
1 BRACE UNDER TOP-7 1/2"x 2'-0" x 7/8" ~
2 TURNED POSTS FROM
2 1/2" SQUARE STOCK ~
2 TRESTLE FEET 11 LONG-
2 1/2" WIDE - 1 1/2" THICK ~
MAIN STRETCHER 1'-7"x 7 1/2"x 1"
NOT INCLUDING TENONS ~
2 GATES 2"x 7/8" STOCK ~

HINGE

SCALE IN INCHES { ELEVATIONS
{ TURNING

31

Trestle-Foot Gate-Leg Table [SEE PLATE 89]

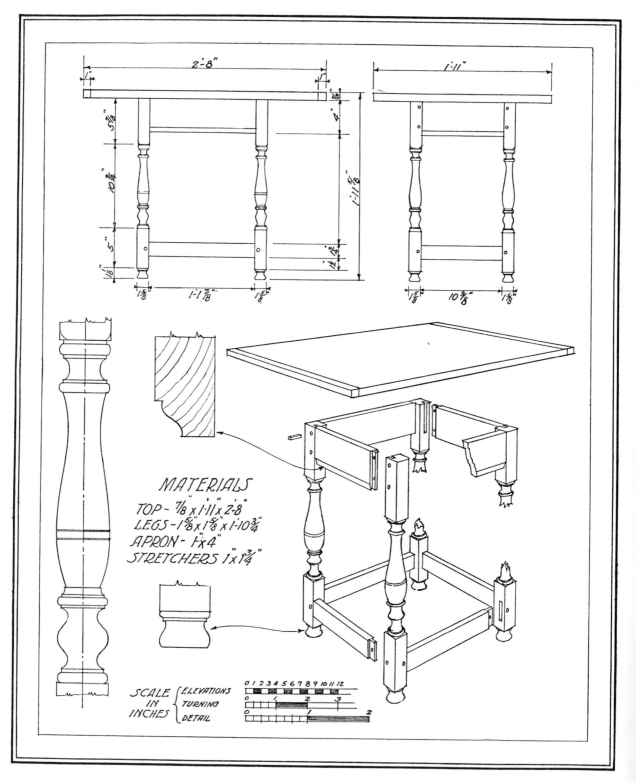

MATERIALS

TOP - ⅞" x 1'-11" x 2'-8"
LEGS - 1⅝" x 1⅝" x 1'-10¾"
APRON - 1" x 4"
STRETCHERS 1" x 1¼"

SCALE IN INCHES { ELEVATIONS / TURNING / DETAIL }

0 1 2 3 4 5 6 7 8 9 10 11 12

3²

All Pine Tavern Table [SEE PLATE 92]

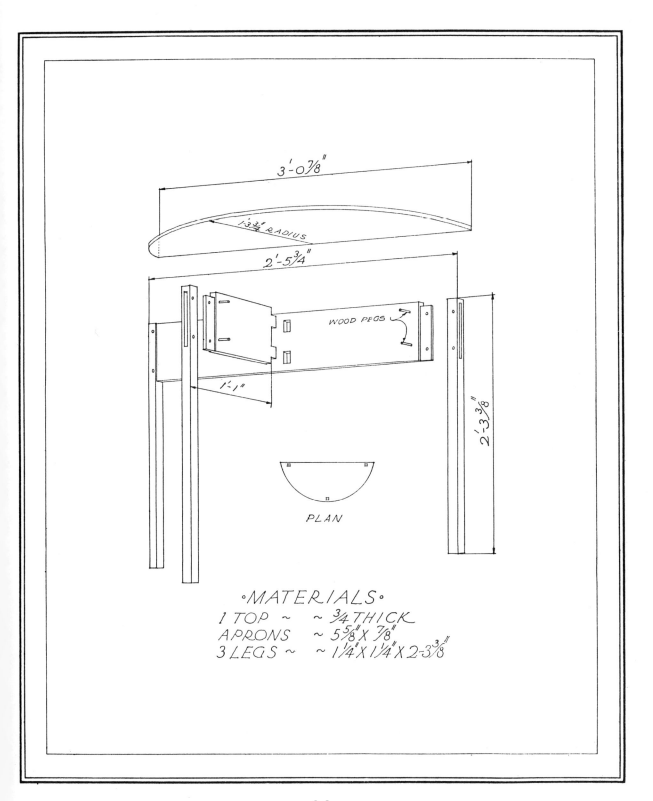

3'-0 7/8"

1'-3 3/4" RADIUS

2'-5 3/4"

WOOD PEGS

1'-1"

2'-3 3/8"

PLAN

·MATERIALS·
1 TOP ~ ~ 3/4 THICK
APRONS ~ 5 5/8" X 7/8"
3 LEGS ~ ~ 1 1/4" X 1 1/4" X 2-3 3/8"

33

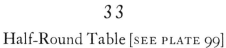

Half-Round Table [SEE PLATE 99]

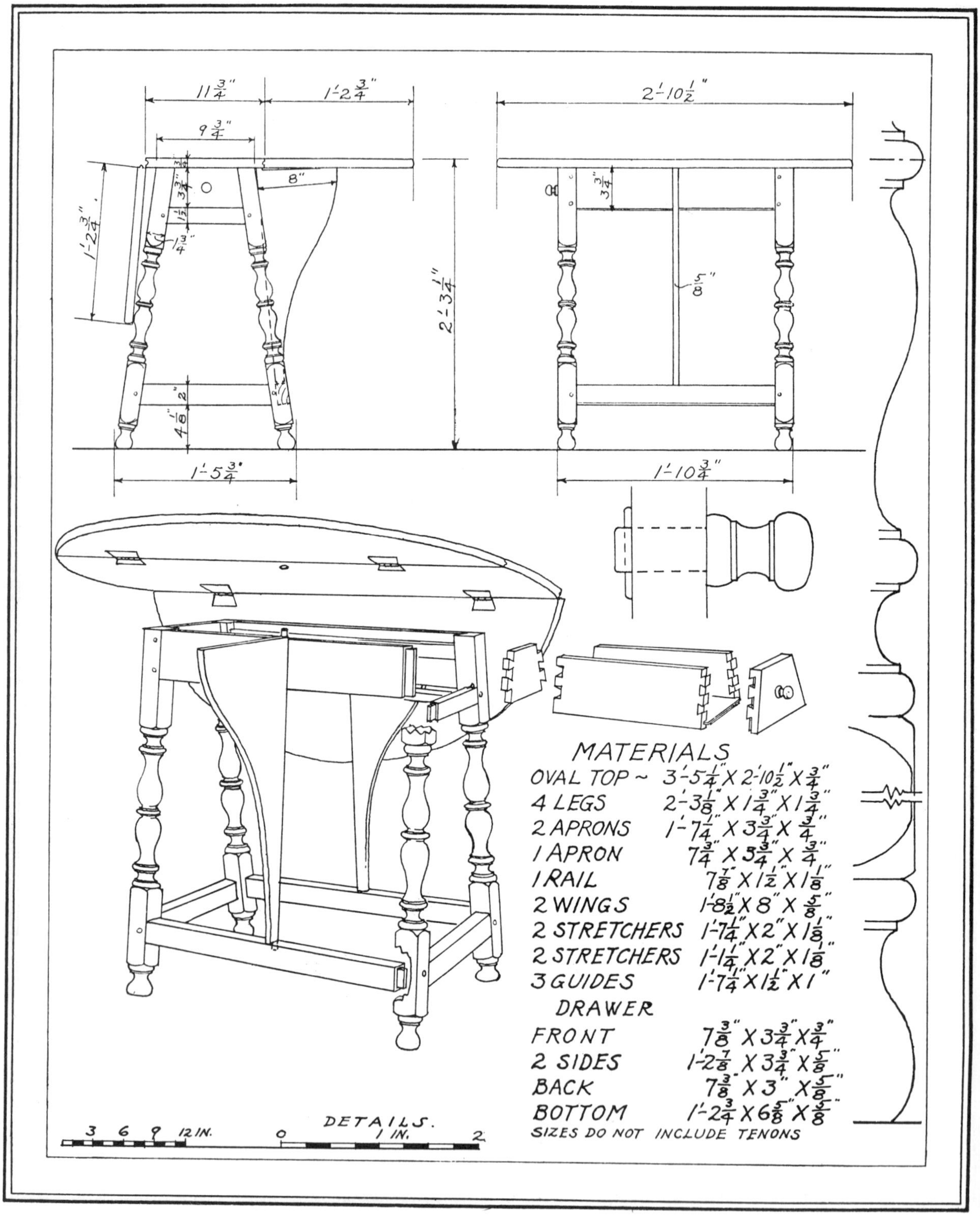
11¾"
1'-2¾"
9¾"
8"
1'-2¾"
2'-10½"
2'-3¼"
¾"
3¾"
1½"
⅝"
2"
4⅛"
1'-5¾"
1'-10¾"
MATERIALS
OVAL TOP ~ 3'-5¼" X 2'-10½" X ¾"
4 LEGS 2'-3⅛" X 1¾" X 1¾"
2 APRONS 1'-7¼" X 3¾" X ¾"
1 APRON 7¾" X 3¾" X ¾"
1 RAIL 7⅞" X 1½" X 1⅛"
2 WINGS 1'-8½" X 8" X ⅝"
2 STRETCHERS 1'-7¼" X 2" X 1⅛"
2 STRETCHERS 1'-1¼" X 2" X 1⅛"
3 GUIDES 1'-7¼" X 1½" X 1"
DRAWER
FRONT 7⅜" X 3¾" X ¾"
2 SIDES 1'-2⅞" X 3¾" X ⅝"
BACK 7⅜" X 3" X ⅝"
BOTTOM 1'-2¾" X 6⅝" X ⅝"
SIZES DO NOT INCLUDE TENONS
3 6 9 12 IN.
DETAILS.
0 1 IN. 2

Maple and Pine Butterfly Table [SEE PLATE 101]

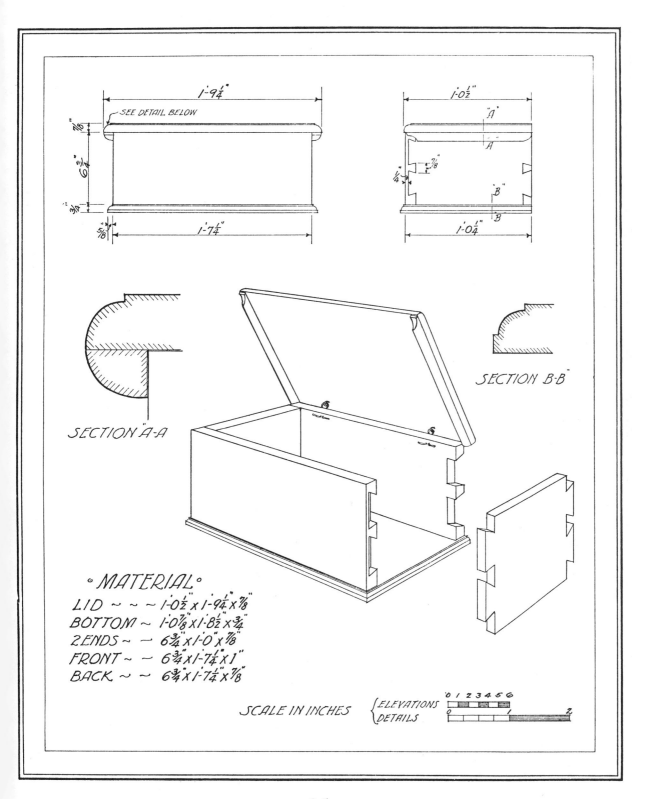

SEE DETAIL BELOW

SECTION "A"-A

SECTION B-B

°MATERIAL°
LID ~ ~ ~ 1'-0½" x 1'-9¼" x ⅞"
BOTTOM ~ 1'-0⅞" x 1'-8½" x ¾"
2 ENDS ~ ~ 6¾" x 1'-0" x ⅞"
FRONT ~ ~ 6¾" x 1'-7¼" x 1"
BACK ~ ~ 6¾" x 1'-7¼" x ⅞"

SCALE IN INCHES

{ELEVATIONS
DETAILS}

0 1 2 3 4 5 6

0   1   2

35

Desk Box [SEE PLATE 102]

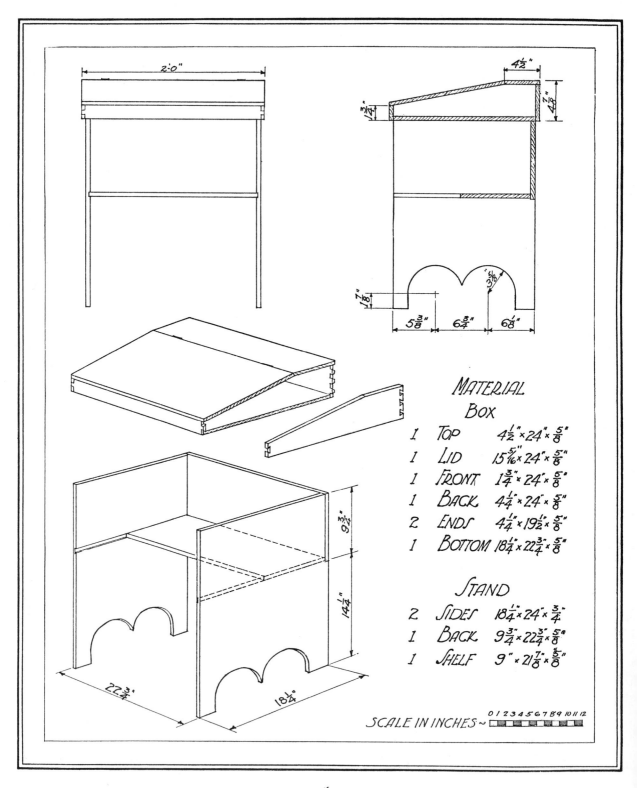

MATERIAL

BOX

1 TOP $4\frac{1}{2}" \times 24" \times \frac{5}{8}"$
1 LID $15\frac{5}{16}" \times 24" \times \frac{5}{8}"$
1 FRONT $1\frac{3}{4}" \times 24" \times \frac{5}{8}"$
1 BACK $4\frac{1}{4}" \times 24" \times \frac{5}{8}"$
2 ENDS $4\frac{1}{4}" \times 19\frac{1}{2}" \times \frac{5}{8}"$
1 BOTTOM $18\frac{1}{4}" \times 22\frac{3}{4}" \times \frac{5}{8}"$

STAND

2 SIDES $18\frac{1}{4}" \times 24" \times \frac{3}{4}"$
1 BACK $9\frac{3}{4}" \times 22\frac{3}{4}" \times \frac{5}{8}"$
1 SHELF $9" \times 21\frac{7}{8}" \times \frac{5}{8}"$

SCALE IN INCHES ~ 0 1 2 3 4 5 6 7 8 9 10 11 12

36

School Desk [SEE PLATE 118]

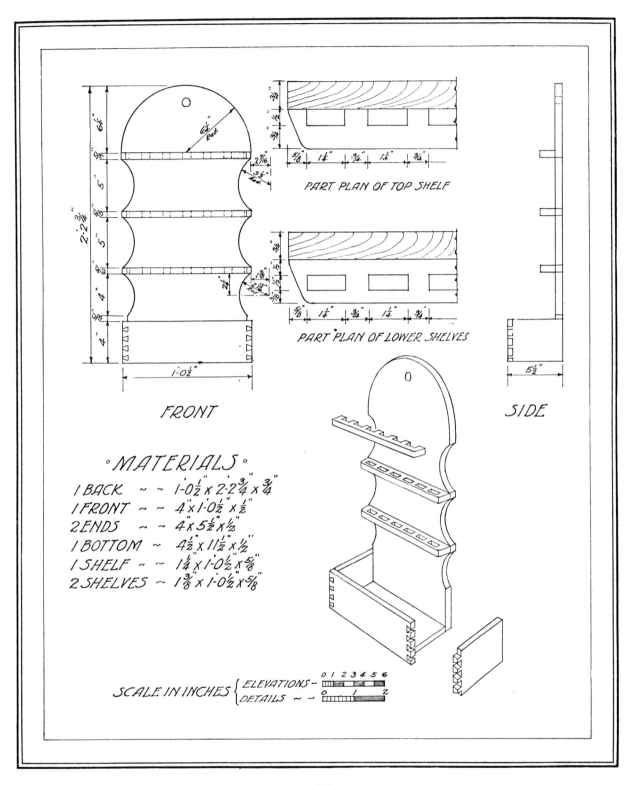

PART PLAN OF TOP SHELF

PART PLAN OF LOWER SHELVES

FRONT

SIDE

MATERIALS

1 BACK	~ ~	$1\text{-}0\frac{1}{2}"\times2\text{-}2\frac{3}{4}"\times\frac{3}{4}"$
1 FRONT	~ ~	$4"\times1\text{-}0\frac{1}{2}"\times\frac{1}{2}"$
2 ENDS	~ ~	$4"\times5\frac{1}{2}"\times\frac{1}{2}"$
1 BOTTOM	~	$4\frac{1}{2}"\times11\frac{1}{2}"\times\frac{1}{2}"$
1 SHELF	~ ~	$1\frac{1}{4}"\times1\text{-}0\frac{1}{2}"\times\frac{5}{8}"$
2 SHELVES	~	$1\frac{3}{8}"\times1\text{-}0\frac{1}{2}"\times\frac{5}{8}"$

SCALE IN INCHES {
ELEVATIONS ~ 0 1 2 3 4 5 6
DETAILS ~ ~ 0 1 2
}

37

Spoon Rack with Box Below [SEE PLATE 121]

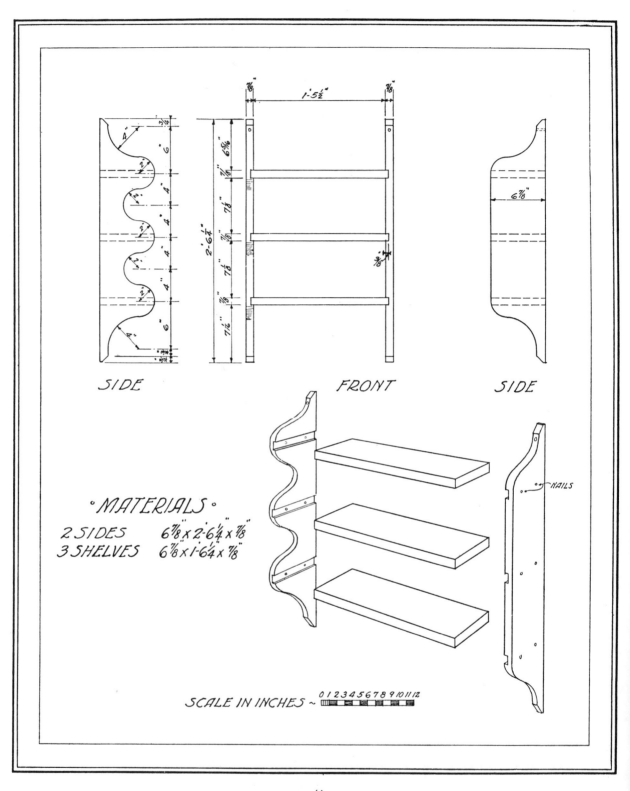

SIDE   FRONT   SIDE

· MATERIALS ·
2 SIDES   6⅞" x 2'-6¼" x ⅞"
3 SHELVES   6⅞" x 1'-6¼" x ⅞"

NAILS

SCALE IN INCHES ~ 0 1 2 3 4 5 6 7 8 9 10 11 12

38

Corner Shelves with One Side Scalloped [SEE PLATE 128]

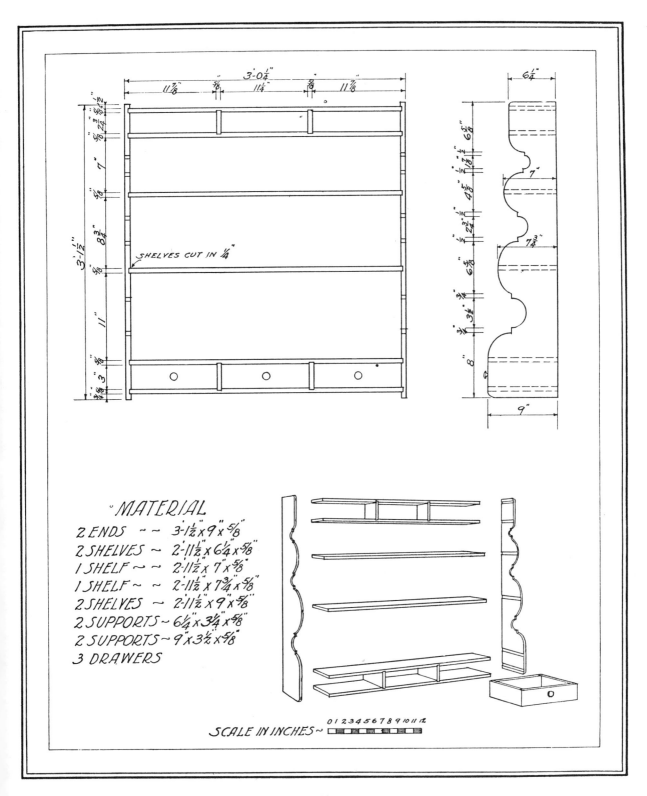

MATERIAL

2 ENDS ~ ~ 3'-1½" x 9" x ⅝"
2 SHELVES ~ 2'-11½" x 6¼" x ⅝"
1 SHELF ~ ~ 2'-11½" x 7" x ⅝"
1 SHELF ~ ~ 2'-11½" x 7¾" x ⅝"
2 SHELVES ~ 2'-11½" x 9" x ⅝"
2 SUPPORTS ~ 6¼" x 3¼" x ⅝"
2 SUPPORTS ~ 9" x 3½" x ⅝"
3 DRAWERS

SHELVES CUT IN ¼"

SCALE IN INCHES ~ 0 1 2 3 4 5 6 7 8 9 10 11 12

39

Shelves with Drawers [SEE PLATE 130]

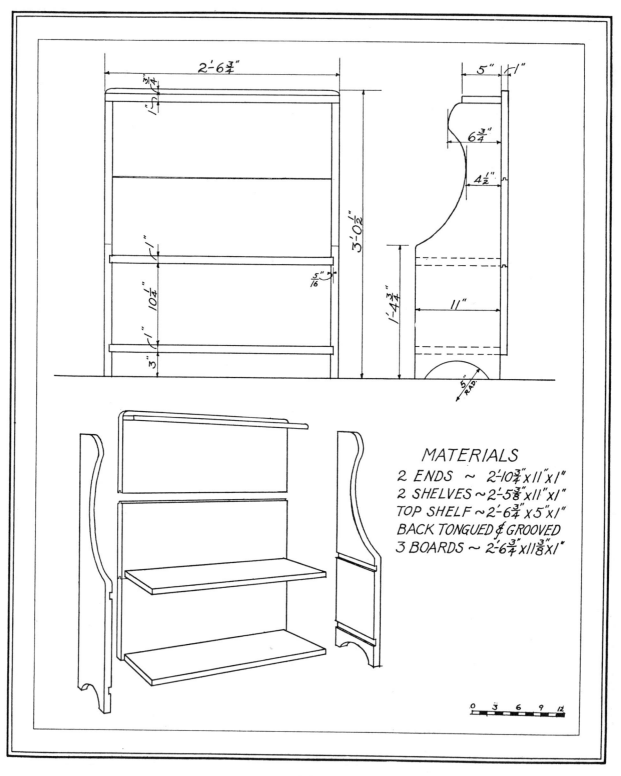

2'-6⅞"

3/4"

1"

3'-0½"

5/16"

1"

10¼"

3"

1"

3"

5"

1"

6¾"

4½"

1'-4¾"

11"

5"
RAD.

MATERIALS

2 ENDS ~ 2'-10¾"×11"×1"
2 SHELVES ~ 2'-5⅜"×11"×1"
TOP SHELF ~ 2'-6¼"×5"×1"
BACK TONGUED & GROOVED
3 BOARDS ~ 2'-6¾"×11⅜"×1"

0   3   6   9   12

40

Small Water Bench [SEE PLATE 131]

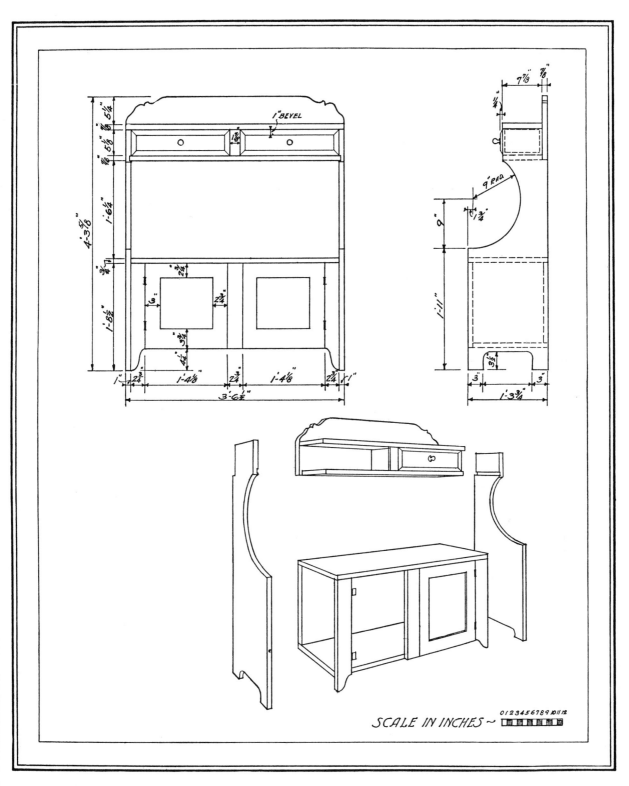

SCALE IN INCHES ~ 0 1 2 3 4 5 6 7 8 9 10 11 12

4I

Water Bench with Drawers and Cupboard [SEE PLATE 132]

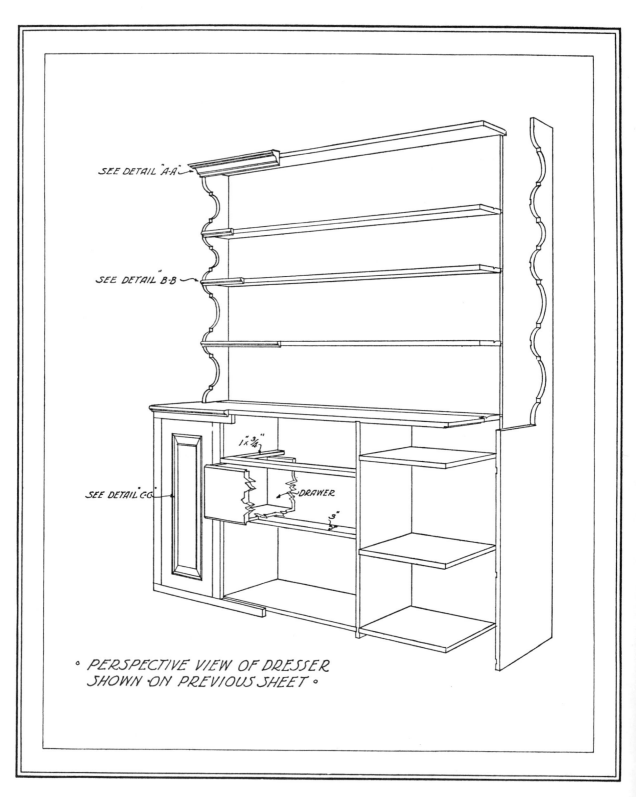

SEE DETAIL "A-A"

SEE DETAIL "B-B"

SEE DETAIL "C-C"

1" x 3/4"

DRAWER

3"

° PERSPECTIVE VIEW OF DRESSER
SHOWN ON PREVIOUS SHEET °

42

Scalloped Dresser with Pennsylvania SlipWare I [SEE PLATE 135]

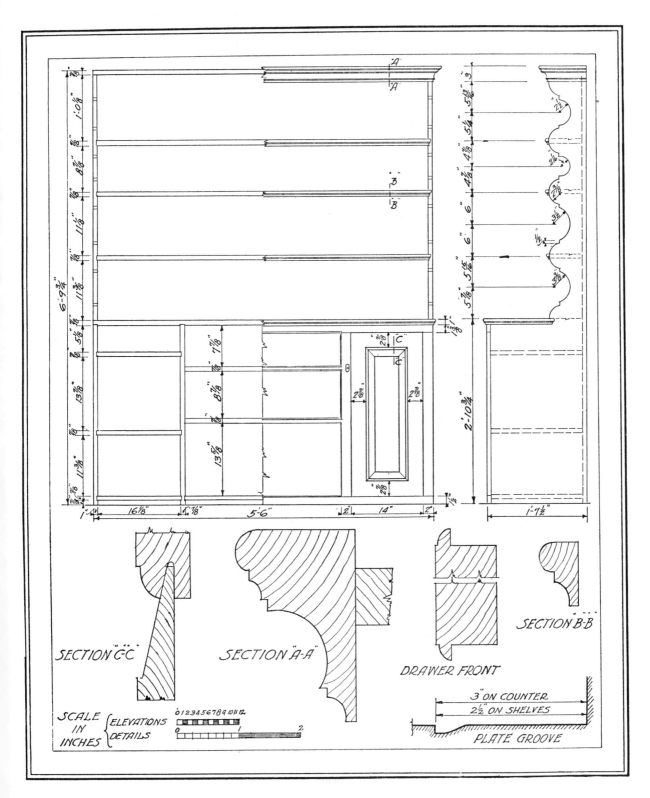

SECTION "C-C"

SECTION "A-A"

SECTION "B-B"

DRAWER FRONT

SCALE IN INCHES { ELEVATIONS DETAILS }

0 1 2 3 4 5 6 7 8 9 10 11 12

0 1 2

3" ON COUNTER
2½" ON SHELVES

PLATE GROOVE

43

Scalloped Dresser with Pennsylvania SlipWare 2 [SEE PLATE 135]

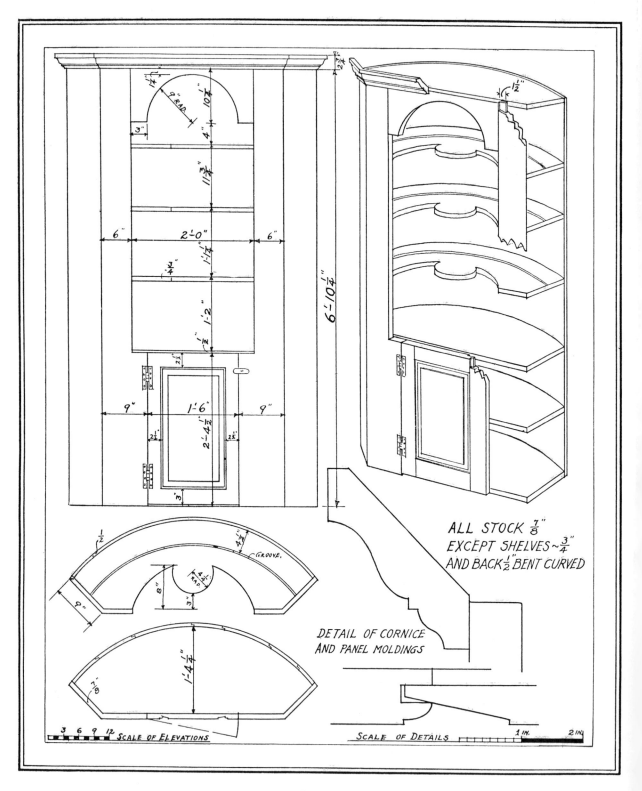

ALL STOCK ⅞" EXCEPT SHELVES ~¾" AND BACK ½" BENT CURVED

DETAIL OF CORNICE AND PANEL MOLDINGS

GROOVE.

3 6 9 12 SCALE OF ELEVATIONS

SCALE OF DETAILS   1 IN.   2 IN.

44

Plain Corner Cupboard with Arched Opening [SEE PLATE 145]

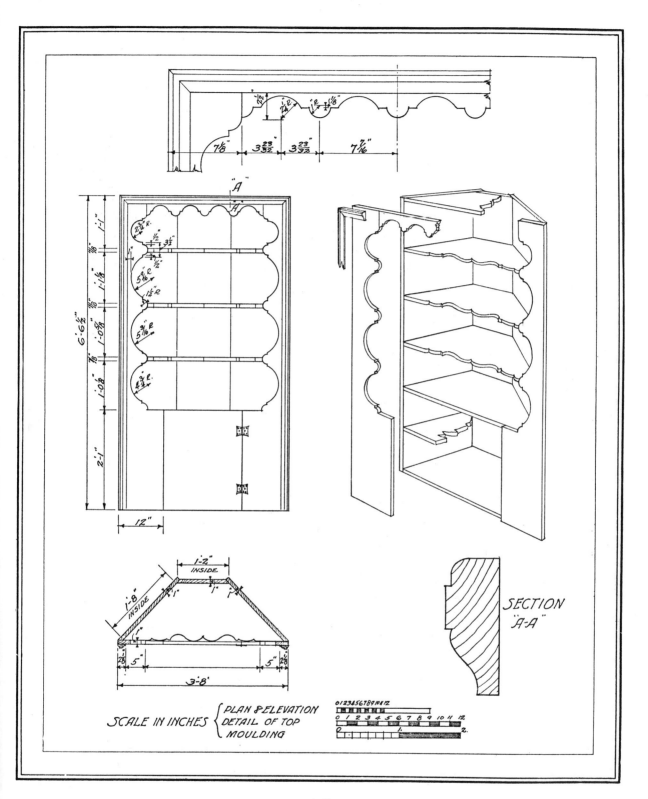

SCALE IN INCHES { PLAN & ELEVATION / DETAIL OF TOP / MOULDING

SECTION "A-A"

45

Scalloped Corner Cupboard with Lustre and China [SEE PLATE 147]

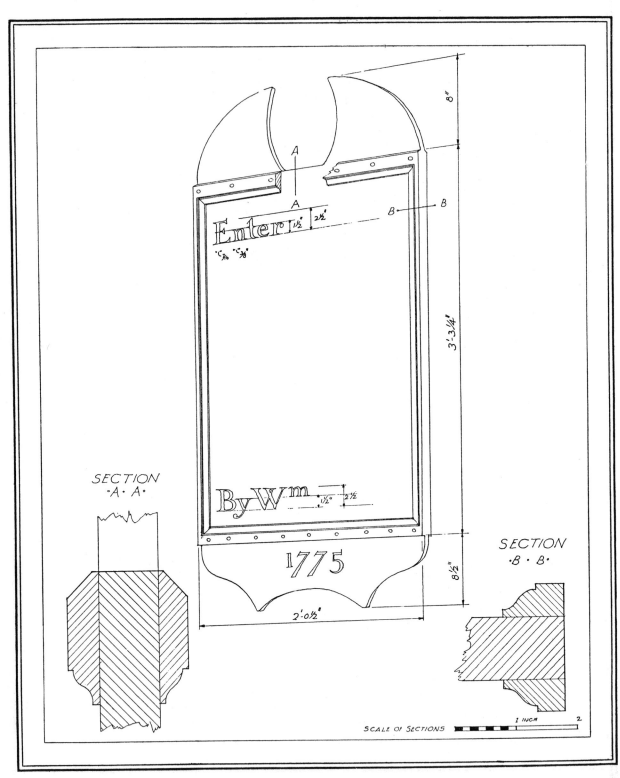

SECTION
·A·A·

SECTION
·B·B·

Enter 1½" 2½"
"C" 7/16 "C" 3/8

By Wm 1½" 2½"

3'-3¼"

8"

8½"

1775

2'-0½"

SCALE of SECTIONS 1 INCH 2

46

Munroe Tavern Sign [SEE PLATE 153]

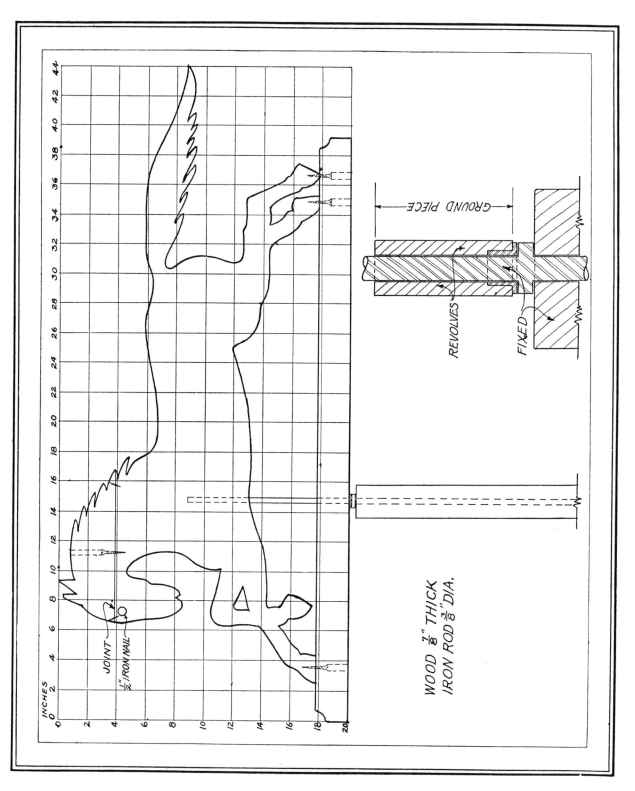

47

Horse Weather Vane [SEE PLATE 162]

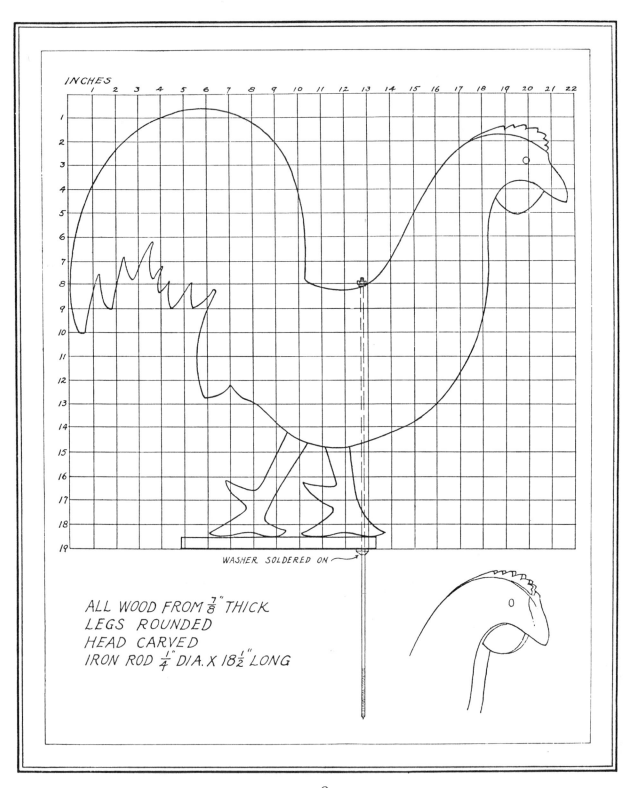

INCHES

ALL WOOD FROM $\frac{7}{8}''$ THICK
LEGS ROUNDED
HEAD CARVED
IRON ROD $\frac{1}{4}''$ DIA. X $18\frac{1}{2}''$ LONG

WASHER SOLDERED ON

48

Rooster Weather Vane [SEE PLATE 164]

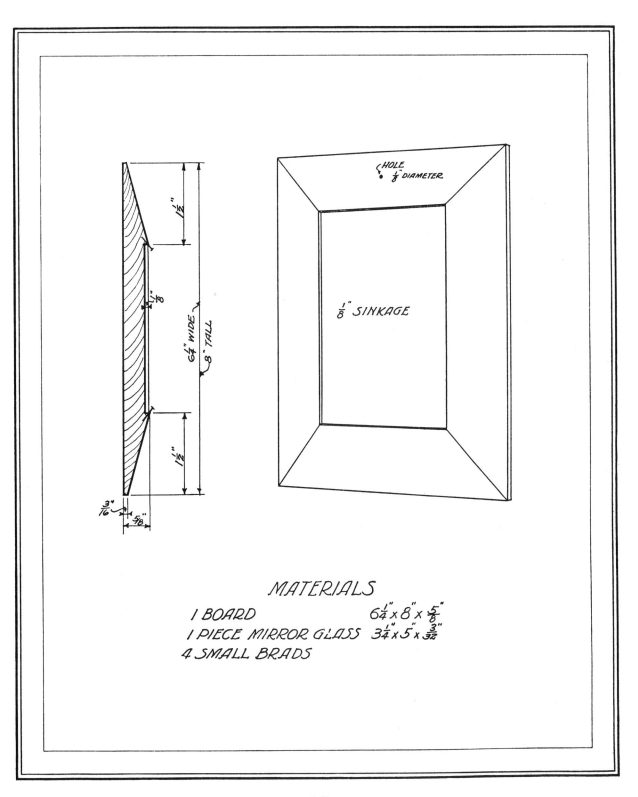

HOLE
⅛" DIAMETER

⅛" SINKAGE

1½"

1⅛"

6¼" WIDE

8" TALL

1½"

3/16"

⅝"

MATERIALS

1 BOARD   6¼" x 8" x ⅝"
1 PIECE MIRROR GLASS   3¼" x 5" x 3/32"
4 SMALL BRADS

49

Plank Mirror [SEE PLATE 171]

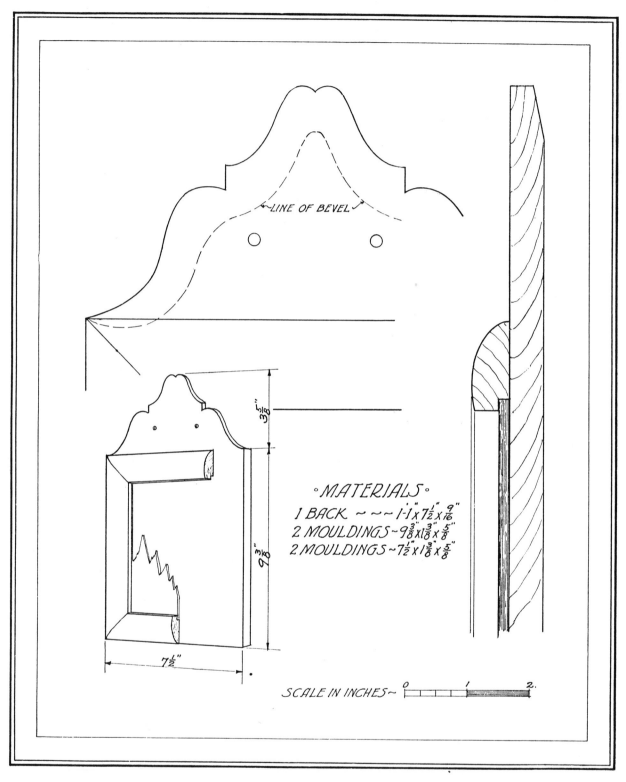

LINE OF BEVEL

°MATERIALS°
1 BACK ~~~ 1·1"x 7½"x 9/16"
2 MOULDINGS ~ 9⅜"x 1⅜"x ⅝"
2 MOULDINGS ~ 7½"x 1⅜"x ⅝"

3⅝"

9⅜"

7½"

SCALE IN INCHES ~ 0   1   2.

50

Very Plain All-Pine Mirror [SEE PLATE 177]

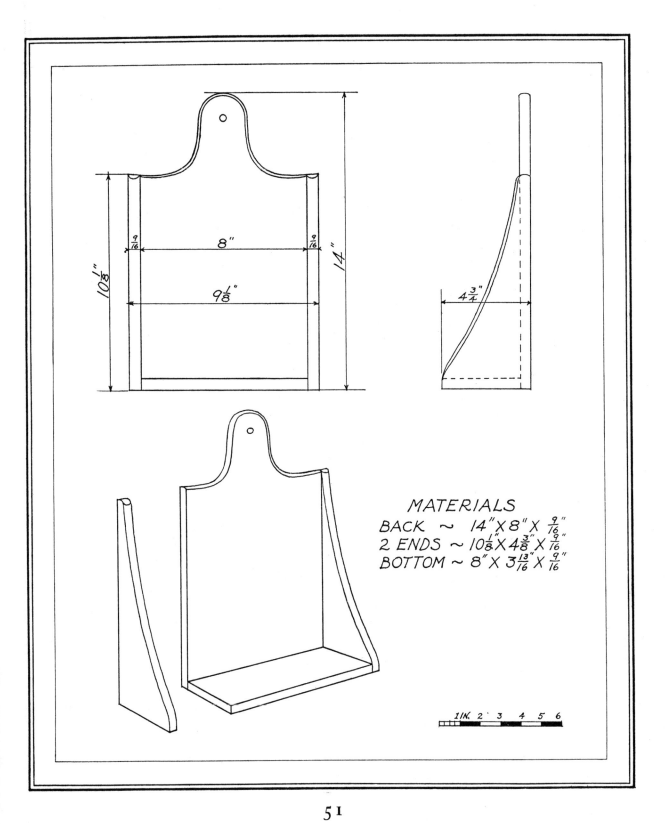

MATERIALS
BACK ~ 14" X 8" X 9/16"
2 ENDS ~ 10 1/8" X 4 3/8" X 9/16"
BOTTOM ~ 8" X 3 13/16" X 9/16"

1 IN. 2 3 4 5 6

5 1

Wall Candle Rest [SEE PLATE 207]

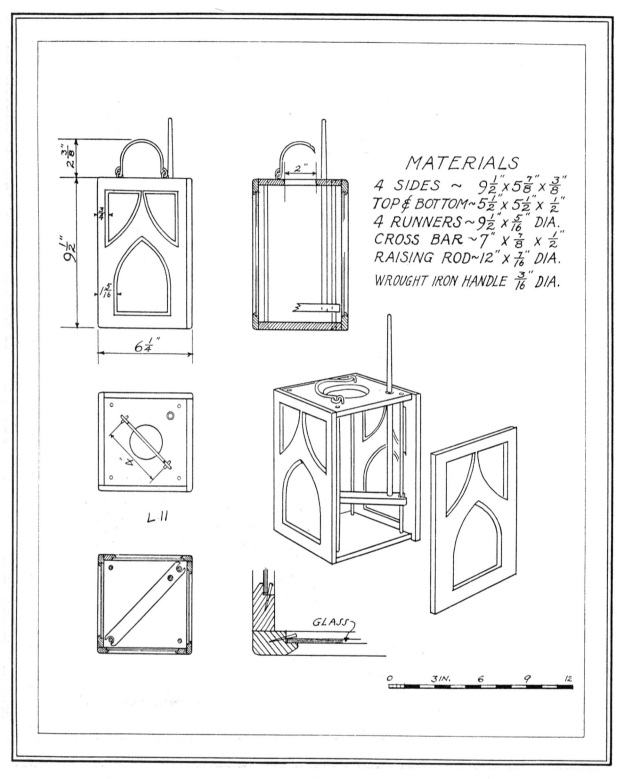

MATERIALS

4 SIDES ~ $9\frac{1}{2}'' \times 5\frac{7}{8}'' \times \frac{3}{8}''$
TOP & BOTTOM ~ $5\frac{1}{2}'' \times 5\frac{1}{2}'' \times \frac{1}{2}''$
4 RUNNERS ~ $9\frac{1}{2}'' \times \frac{5}{16}''$ DIA.
CROSS BAR ~ $7'' \times \frac{7}{8}'' \times \frac{1}{2}''$
RAISING ROD ~ $12'' \times \frac{7}{16}''$ DIA.
WROUGHT IRON HANDLE $\frac{3}{16}''$ DIA.

GLASS

L 11

$0 \quad 3$ IN. $\quad 6 \quad 9 \quad 12$

52

Gothic Lantern [SEE PLATE 209]

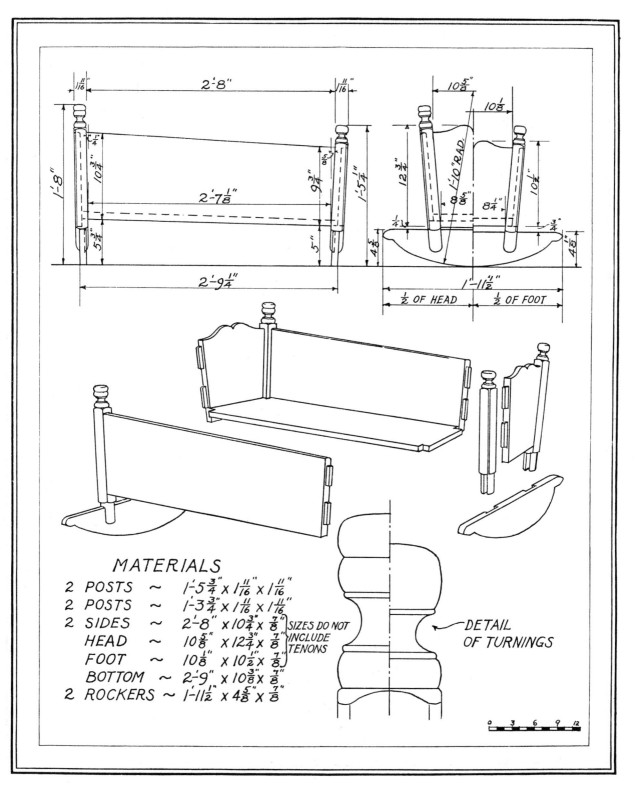

MATERIALS

2 POSTS ~ $1'-5\frac{3}{4}'' \times 1\frac{11}{16}'' \times 1\frac{11}{16}''$
2 POSTS ~ $1'-3\frac{3}{4}'' \times 1\frac{11}{16}'' \times 1\frac{11}{16}''$
2 SIDES ~ $2'-8'' \times 10\frac{3}{4}'' \times \frac{7}{8}''$ SIZES DO NOT
HEAD ~ $10\frac{5}{8}'' \times 12\frac{3}{4}'' \times \frac{7}{8}''$ INCLUDE
FOOT ~ $10\frac{1}{8}'' \times 10\frac{1}{2}'' \times \frac{7}{8}''$ TENONS
BOTTOM ~ $2'-9'' \times 10\frac{3}{8}'' \times \frac{7}{8}''$
2 ROCKERS ~ $1'-11\frac{1}{2}'' \times 4\frac{5}{8}'' \times \frac{7}{8}''$

DETAIL
OF TURNINGS

53

Rocking Cradle with Turned Posts [SEE PLATE 218]

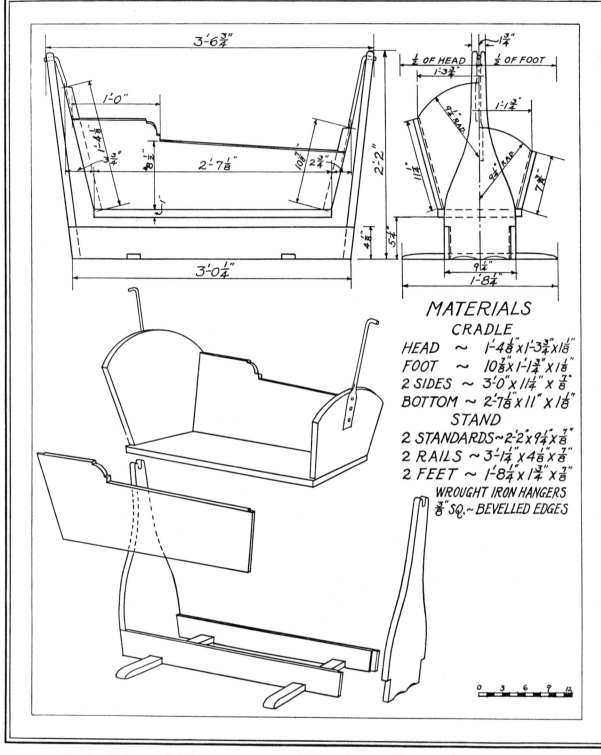

MATERIALS

CRADLE

HEAD ~ $1'\text{-}4\frac{1}{8}''$ x $1'\text{-}3\frac{3}{4}''$ x $1\frac{1}{8}''$
FOOT ~ $10\frac{7}{8}''$ x $1'\text{-}1\frac{3}{4}''$ x $1\frac{1}{8}''$
2 SIDES ~ $3'\text{-}0''$ x $1\frac{1}{4}''$ x $\frac{7}{8}''$
BOTTOM ~ $2'\text{-}7\frac{1}{8}''$ x $11''$ x $1\frac{1}{8}''$

STAND

2 STANDARDS ~ $2'\text{-}2''$ x $9\frac{1}{4}''$ x $\frac{7}{8}''$
2 RAILS ~ $3'\text{-}1\frac{1}{4}''$ x $4\frac{1}{8}''$ x $\frac{7}{8}''$
2 FEET ~ $1'\text{-}8\frac{1}{4}''$ x $1\frac{3}{4}''$ x $\frac{7}{8}''$

WROUGHT IRON HANGERS
$\frac{3}{8}''$ SQ. ~ BEVELLED EDGES

54

Swinging Cradle with Trestle Feet [SEE PLATE 222]

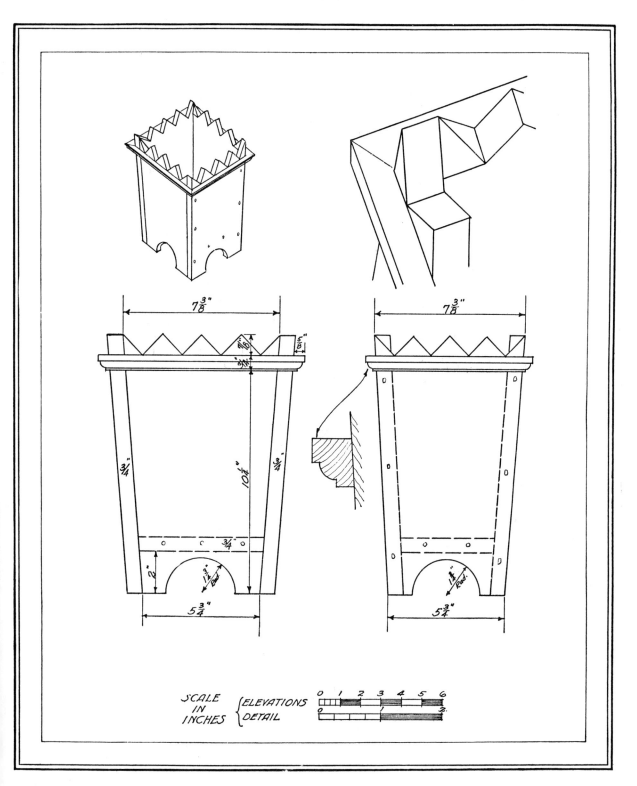

Scale in inches
{Elevations
{Detail

0 1 2 3 4 5 6

55

Plant Box [SEE PLATE 225]

A SHORT LIST OF BOOKS AND MUSEUMS

FOR FURTHER study of this subject I suggest reference to the following books and publications: Herbert Cescinsky, *English Furniture of the Eighteenth Century*, *The Old World House*, and *English and American Furniture;* Herbert Cescinsky and Ernest R. Gribble, *Early English Furniture and Woodwork;* Charles Over Cornelius, *Early American Furniture;* Frank Cousins and P. M. Riley, *The Wood-Carver of Salem;* George Francis Dow, *Domestic Life in New England in the Seventeenth Century*, *The Arts and Crafts in New England, 1704-1775: Gleanings from Newspapers;* Walter Alden Dyer, *Early American Craftsmen;* Alice Morse Earle, *Stage-Coach and Tavern Days;* Norman Morrison Isham and Albert F. Brown, *Early Connecticut Houses*, *Early Rhode Island Houses;* Fiske Kimball, *Domestic Architecture of the American Colonies and of the Early Republic;* Luke Vincent Lockwood, *Colonial Furniture in America;* Irving Whitall Lyon, *Colonial Furniture of New England;* Donald Millar, *Colonial Furniture: Measured Drawings*, *Measured Drawings of Some Colonial and Georgian Houses;* Wallace Nutting, *Furniture of the Pilgrim Century;* Publications of the South Kensington Museum, London; *Old-Time New England: The Bulletin of the Society for the Preservation of New England Antiquities;* Esther Singleton, *Furniture of Our Forefathers;* and to the following museums: The Rhode Island School of Design at Providence, The Morgan Memorial Museum at Hartford, The Essex Institute at Salem, The Antiquarian Society at Concord, the many museum houses of the Society for the Preservation of New England Antiquities, the Boston Museum of Fine Arts, and the Metropolitan Museum of Art.